A BOOK OF
PSALMS

EDWARD
CLARKE

PARACLETE PRESS
BREWSTER, MASSACHUSETTS

Paraclete Poetry Series Editor
Mark S. Burrows

2020 First Printing

A Book of Psalms

Copyright © 2020 by Edward Clarke

ISBN 978-1-64060-357-8

The Paraclete Press name and logo (dove on cross) are trademarks of Paraclete Press, Inc.

Library of Congress Control Number:2019956462

10 9 8 7 6 5 4 3 2 1

Published by Paraclete Press
Brewster, Massachusetts
www.paracletepress.com

Printed in the United States of America

Contents

BOOK THREE

BOOK FOUR

Preface

If someone were to ask me why I wrote this book, I might be tempted to quote Meister Eckhart to say that these poems have been made 'in order that God may be born in the soul and the soul be born in God', although I may not always have realized it while writing them. If it was for this birth that, as Eckhart says, 'the whole of Scripture was written and why God created the whole world', then I see that art has a part to play in the delivery. It can help to bring those eternal things to a kind of completion in our consciousness: the character of the birth might have everything to do with the words and images of poetry as it engages with the 'Word' and 'Image' of the Bible.

These poems are not translations or versifications of the Psalms. They are conversations with, and hesitations about, these ancient texts: sometimes 'imitations as unruly as | My sons', as I complain in my unruly imitation of Psalm 80. In the spirit of Psalm 1, they are always transplantations.

Although I have worked my way through the Masoretic Text (MT), consulting old concordances and lexicons, in making these poems my Bible is the King James Version and its foundational sixteenth-century translations. Unfortunately, I am the first generation not to have grown up with the old *Book of Common Prayer* in church and so Miles Coverdale's translation of the Psalms is less familiar to me than our revised versions of it. Donald Davie has rightly emphasized that any late modern engagement with the Bible must remember the 'suffering and dying' involved in the early modern translations.

The poems are numbered according to the arrangement of Psalms in the MT and the KJV. I look on the superscriptions in the original, relating texts to David, the sons of Korah, Asaph, and others, as clues to the divine structure of the whole, and my poems have been written with them as guides.

The cover of this book is an image that lies behind my version of Psalm 144: Michelangelo's representation of Daniel on the Sistine Chapel ceiling. In my poem the two cherubim who play about the prophet are not strange children but conceived of as my two sons who have grown up through my making of these poems.

Book one

1 🙊 # A Tree

And as he passed this way one evening,
Murmuring no hymn
I'd learned at school, the pavement screaming
Its wide advice around him,
Like crowds with in-ear head-
Phones howling, he
Stopped dead and saw some men seated,
Discoursing ironically.

Follow me, he said, his hand
As massive as
The marble hand of David: stand
And make my crooked tracks
Perceptible, he seemed
To me to say,
And I arose and followed, dreamed
He was with me this way.

Prosperous is that man, or blessed with joy,
Who has not walked through streets and fields of his day
In agitated company, nor does
He stand around at entrances with those
That breathe out smoke and swear there's nothing higher
Than an endless play of signifiers,
Nor will he sit through meetings with bosses that scoff at
The very syllabi they'd sell for a profit.
But his delight is in the burden of
His lust, the massive self-secluding love
The everlasting has for us, and on
This law, whose words a finger cast at stone
That rain has made illegible, he makes
His heartfelt moan, a murmuring cry that breaks
Its sound upon his tongue by day and sundown.

And like a tree transplanted to a land
More arid than mine through whose ground a river
Is ramified, it falls out he'll deliver
In season fruit from leaves as yet umbrageous,
And whatsoever he makes is efficacious.
Not so the people lost on every street,
But they are chaff winds blow in their disquiet.
Therefore, the faithless do not arise and stand
In the moment: sinners crowd no righteous man.
There's something that re-routes the way of the righteous:
The self-metaled way a standstill of the faithless.

2 ❦ The Soil

I

Why have the nations met to make uproar?
Everyone is muttering about nothing,
Or posting in vain,
Against God and his anointed one.
A referendum came,
And word is: 'We'll lift restraints,
Cut from us the cord.'

He that lives at the limits of mine eye
Laughs in scorn, will speak to them at last,
And flare the sky
With divine, burning anger, anger
Exclusively divine:
'But I anoint the king that's mine
On my holy mountain of Zion.'

God said to me, 'You are among my sons,
I have delivered you, now ask for your
                              Inheritance,
            And I will give you nations to break
                  Under a rod's iron sounds:
            For your possessions, all earth's ends,
                  To smash as porcelains.'

Now of all times, be disciplined by prudence.
Cultivate, you billionaires, world leaders
                        Of nation states,
            Your fear of God, rejoice in trembling,
                  Embrace the son who waits
            At all stand-stills, whose anger abates:
                  Prosperous those moved thence.

                              II
            Jesus died with a Psalm on his lips
            And now we live in that mystery:
            A line of personal lament
            To lay the seed of our histories.

            Elaborate laws and canticles,
            Translations of corrupted texts
            For coronation rituals,
            Provide the salts the root collects:

            Like frail eggshells in fresh-made soil,
            Long lines of ancient lineages
            Lie part buried, look almost unspoiled,
            In all subsequent languages.

            Even now the very absence of purpose
            In royal Psalms out of context
            Makes a kind of soil of them
            Without which nothing can come next.

3 ⅋ Rejection
Of David

It took exactly a year and a day
As if the news were hung with charms:
They wrote kindly to say, the very hour
I finished the Penitential Psalms,
That they had had to pass on them.
It seemed like time to start again
And ask, how they're increased that trouble me,
How many am I up against?

I wrote those lines two springs ago,
And now I see how necessary
Was that rejection of my manuscript,
How I had needed then a hairy
Raiment, so to speak, to cry
Absurdly in the wilderness
Their lack of interest had opened up:
The space where I awoke and was blessed.

4 ⅋ Resolution
Of David

I woke, I cried, propped up inside
The crowding hours, as if I slept
With those that sleep and drink beside the Court,
The homeless over whom I've stepped
Countless mornings in a rush.
But then I thought, that Psalm's selected
For matins, this for compline: change your tone,
Awake, rise up, sustained, protected.

How can a tidied line sustain me?
When I'll have found myself alone,

Empty at dawn or chronically drunk on life,
	Without a bed, without my home:
	When I am dead, not yet gone, and trapped
	Inside distress, inside my cries,
My glory turned to shame, a son of man
	Made up of vanity and lies.

	Cry hard enough, you're set apart,
	A room's enlarged inside of you,
And there kindness is curled and upside down,
	Calmly poised to be thrust through.
	You'll tremble at his future cries
	He'll mumble to your heart in bed.
His smile shall delight us more than wine: we shall lay
	Him down when he is quieted.

5 ❧ May Blossom
Of David

	Open an ear already open,
	And drown your eyes, to read my words.
	Mouth these murmuring meditations:
	The voice of my cry is meant to be heard.
In the morning my voice is driven: I mark the rows.
	In the morning the sun leans out and sows.

	Our times have grown up insincere
	And each of us deserves some scorn:
	We lie like soil ungrateful to sight
	And must be turned to be reborn.
The light that ploughs the morning stars now drives
	Its share through unidealized lives.

Since I am all of them that lie,
Of lies I built your house and grounds,
And hope that you shall come and stay,
That in my lines your truth abounds:
Upon the tongue's smoothed flags my feet have slipped
From throat's fresh grave I reach for lips.

While earth remains, seedtime and harvest,
Turn over my mundanity:
Bury the heart's imaginations
Under their roots' fertility.
I hear beyond white hedges of neighbouring farms
No shepherd's far-off songs or Psalms.

6 ⧫ ## A Penitential Psalm
Of David

O God, don't bollock me in anger,
Don't rebuke me hotly,
Stoop, God, over my sunken state,
Splint, God, my bones that shake:
My soul shakes greatly,
And you, God, how much longer?

Return to me, airlift my soul,
Save me for sake of kindness,
Or just because in death there's no
Memento that I know:
Inside the blindness
Of earth just earth to hold.

I flood my couch with heavy tears
And make my bed high seas:
I swim to gasping point by night,
My eyes without eyesight,
Like enemies
That rain archaic spears.

Stop making trouble, and God receives
    The cry of my tears, and God
Receives my prayer, and God has heard
    His song: let all I feared
        Shake as a wood
        That turns against seared leaves.

7 ⟡ **The Root of Lion** (Version IV)
Of David

    And yet another version's plucked
To bits in the maw of this one, whose origin's
Unknown, like all cognates of *lion*: their Latin
    Word lies and marks our foragings,
        Its root ready to spring,
        A word that would rend its thing.

    Were you conceived in these lines I have
Revised, and born astride this poem of ours,
Your face might be a language to take my own,
    That's seen in dreams and odd things, the hours
        I've spent mumbling at dawn,
        At its insatiable yawn.

    Arise in anger, rouse yourself:
My words encircle you, would goad you to
Your rampant height, and would be judged, or torn
    Apart eternally, by you,
        In time, whose holes reflect
        Revisions you'd reject.

8 ⁊ *Noli me tangere*
Of David

You are the man that balanced a hoe,
In fingers of April showers,
Ordaining bright May flowers:
The shade a woman turned to see, that bid
Her hold him fast and not let go,
To have dominion over, not fear to see,
The wolf, the bear, the lion, and that which hid
Its steps and toes to walk through paths of the sea.

And yet the things which we have heard
Run out as broken vessels
Upon forgotten missals
Under our feet: they break like schemes of rhyme
Through layers of verses to flower in the word.
Their meaning's dense inside us, folded up
Like cloth of starlight at the end of time,
In beaks of birds, in case we let it slip.

9–10 ⁊ Never Tell Me
Of David

I

The voice that speaks this Psalm
Is at the gates of death
And almost seems too calm
In face of what is left:
It might be war-torn Syria,
Aleppo yesterday,
The mass of man's hysteria
Behind the words we pray.
Some say it's about the exile,
Others, Goliath confounded,
And every ruin's a pile

Of cities before they're founded.
The devastation's hid
Behind the words of praise
In houses in my head
These realistic days.
It is the absence of singing
The Book of Common Prayer
In my impoverished upbringing
That makes me now despair
Of common rites and art:
I see a city wrecked
By fighters in my heart
And almost nothing's left.

Shall the poor be always forgotten?
Our patient abiding perish?
If the core you reach is rotten
There's still its pips to cherish.
Up, up, and let not man,
Sunk down in the hole he's made,
Have the upper hand.

II

Why do you stand far off, a silent double?
And hide your face these needful times of trouble?
The ungodly like the sun, so practical
        And prevalent, have spread their hell
Across the world to persecute the poor:
        Let them be taken by smart devices
        That they imagined with their divisive
Philosophy, the machine that must have more.

Lamenting I hadn't written acrostically,
I scanned my capitals prophetically,
And found the very word I want right now,
        'Sprung up and unafraid' somehow,
Spelt by the final lines of section one:

I use that section's final words
I since crossed out to show I heard
The ungodly has said in my heart, I am not cast down.

He sits in the thievish corners of my lines
And welcomes the old inside allusion's dens,
He lurks as a lion in quasi-rhymes and mauls
The roaming hunter, or fawns, or falls:
I stop and find I am by thoughts surprised.
He has said in my heart that word I caught
That's full of cursing, deceit and fraud,
The word that's no word for censorious eyes.

Take away ungodliness, what's left?
A man of earth that's woken by the theft:
A hand arises, pulls its arm across
A wall's apocalyptic grass,
Its lines made of a name that's only found
Inside its opposite inside
These lines of mine, and I shall hide
In heavy lines a voice of excised sound.

11 ❧ Manuscript Materials
Of David

Oppressed by sons of mine that cannot lie,
By thoughts of lines, imperious and in need,
The thought of looking them back in the eye
And saying no when they might scream or plead,
I opened up a book of photographs
Of crossings out and re-imaginings
From clues in rhymes, an older master's drafts,
To see how faults are made at last to sing:
I saw an arrow lead from one rough start
To deft refinements on the facing page,

Those pages now a thousand miles apart,
The loose leaves of a notebook scattered in age.
This song still flees my noisy sons downstream
And puts its trust in its uprearing dream.

12 ❦ *Il Mare*
Of David

The help I need might take the form of a note,
Or paradox, a future tenant's left
                    On quitting this house, which I
Mistook for one the former owner wrote,
To let us know a forwarding address
                    And say a farewell 'Hi',
                    Apprise us of a quirk
                    Or two the house has not,
                    I see, developed as yet:
A thing I've now mislaid in heaps of work.

One possible scenario, I've seen,
Is that this paradox, this glimpse of the future,
                    Sparks off a love affair,
As notes are exchanged across a mutual dream
Of time, a kind of holy gap or suture,
                    A hope two stories share:
                    Such faith shall make you wait
                    Inside our world of lies
                    For that which purifies
Heartfelt clichés to words more pale of late.

13 ❧ 'Lo vers mi porta, Corona'
Of David

How long was it you said you're going to be?
    How long a line or stanza?
How long will you forget I am forever
    About to hear your answer?

How long will you conceal from me your face
    Inside typology:
That smile, which loves to turn itself away
    In etymology?

Scan this language I couldn't help but learn:
    It can't be mine to keep.
Let my eyes be light in case I am
    Dismembered in my sleep.

Hear me in case this form says, I've prevailed,
    Rejoicing at my fall:
I put my content in it lovingly
    As I would box a ball.

My heart rejoices at the prospect of
    Its safe delivery:
But I must wander way behind and trust
    Someone sings it for me.

14 (and 53) ❧ The Idiot's Guide
Of David

The fool has taken to heart an *Idiot's Guide*,
The fool has said in his heart, there is no God:
    They are perplexed,
They say that meaning's functional, that cat
Is cat because it isn't cap or bat.

The fool rejects
Mysterious immanence of meaning in signs:
The iconic language we speak, the Word that shines
                    As things do through it.
I read an *Idiot's Guide* to get this straight,
To prove we are today all apostate,
                    Or complex, or fluid.
The substance of these words presents to me
An almost duplicate identity
                    To hammer home
This point that we've betrayed the truth, the Word
That's nailed to metaphors, its trace deferred
                    In time that's flown.
Have all the workers of iniquity
No knowledge? Scientific certainty
                    (Our love, or lack,
Of it) eats up the people as we eat bread,
And on their flight the dead forget to dread
                    A righteous hijack.
The truth's betrayed by fools, by all of us
On earth, so we can build ourselves its house
                    Of many mansions,
Without our knowing even the building's begun,
The better to fulfill the inscrutable plan
                    Creation sanctions:
That man must recreate himself the Word
In which he lives: the world that loves our words.

15 ⁊ **The Pilgrim**
Of David

And who shall tarry archaically
            When day is far spent here?
And who shall rest tonight upon
            The nearby hemisphere?

I wish for him who wakes next morning
To walk another stretch:
I'll serve him from my cool, dark heart
Old words I shall have fetched.

I thought I'd beg or steal his shoes
Before he goes tomorrow:
My heart and mind two tiny stones
To put in what I'll borrow.
I have no doubt he'll shake them out
A few steps from this place,
But I'll become myself again
And gaze upon his face.

16 ⁂ The Sliver
Of David

I am asleep inside a night of stories,
Under a spell that's still to be blessed,
And ashes sprout
Like words throughout
These silent grounds, my mind at rest:
Hedge me with flowering thorn and birds of faerie
Shall look askance about their nest.

What can this mean? Was he who dreamt of me
Filled with the Holy Ghost or just
Wired on new wine
The hour of prime?
These days the Spirit's poured on dust
And men like willows dream their prophecy
On mirrored leaves a girl adjusts.

17 ☙ The Spindle
Of David

Suppose I say or chant a Psalm,
What is it I've recited?
A tale that turns into the tale
An old man tells inside it,
Which caused a curious prince to quit his hunting
And make the happy ending.

I cannot lie, the lips I've used
To say these lines are lips
I've used to lie; my feet have slipped
From pencil and fingertips:
Hide me under your wings and I shall take
Your face when I awake.

To begin at all is to taste the apple
Of the eye, to touch the end
Of a spindle, and fall down dead asleep,
And dream of who can mend
And who can measure in words this rift in time,
The old tale that I am.

18 ☙ Flight
Of David

I

Already confident in its distress,
I found a cry inside my ears,
A cry that took my lines and nets
To cast all night along its floods of tears:
Earth shook and moved,
Potentially,
Foundations shook and were removed,
I might discover out at sea.

A wind picked up along its ancient sayings
        Like thoughts or something looked upon
        Immediately heard in the songs they're playing
On air this morning: a thick pavilion
                Shined about
                Like stanzas broken
        On high, a cherub ridden out
        Like messages acrostically spoken.

I wondered, should I pull a line from out
        Each stanza, mend it, make another,
        When at your word, and still in doubt,
My nets were broken by a force discovered
                Below the straits:
                A multitude
        That's brought into a larger place
        And gasps at its infinitude.

Imagination kindles in its room,
        The cry's old voice inside its ear:
        The sky behind the afternoon
Is loosed in thunder it takes me years to hear,
                And underfoot
                Suddenly
        There's nothing but a word whose root
        Is 'drop', a sky made up of sea.

                        II
He that flies upon the wings of the wind
        Becomes a storm of ocean squalls
Deposited on streets through which I wind
        My way to work, a line recalled
                Glanced at, ignored,
                Which once had soared,
        A branch of leaves against the wall.

The street is strewn with famous phrases torn
    By skies from freshly heavy trees,
My awe becomes compassionate, transformed
    By sights a fallen rider sees:
                Clouds, which once ranged,
                Now beg for change,
        Recumbent under crowds new born.

His sight shall light my candle, make me light,
    And make my feet like chamois feet
To set me scraping to a rugged height,
    A steep horizon's stones my street.
                Enlarge my steps,
                I cannot slip:
        The world shall fall under my feet.

His hand teaches on high my hand to write,
    My arms archaically to break
An anecdotal style that's put to flight,
    To tread its neck to dust winds take.
                In him I've slept
                And words have leapt
        Over the words that made us great.

19 ⅋ ## The Skylight
Of David

                            I
Invention woke inside an attic space
As if there came a sound of rushing day.
A sonnet called *The Skylight*'s not as close
As was that room of rhymes misplaced, or said
Internally without a sound, inside,
Let's say, the next line's breathless present tense,
Which must be running late or thinking to hide
In crowds that press the opened door of sense.

These rhymes have climbed the text and hauled, it seems,
Invention with his bed upon the slates
And let him down, while he still lies and dreams,
Into the midst of the broken open space,
And as they press, peer in, predictably talk,
Day says to day, take up thy bed and walk.

II

Your topic always was this ancient text
And how you woke inside it, on the lines
Of its horizon, beside a few bent pegs
And stones around scorched ground, a pool that shines.
It is a place that turned into a room
Or canopy or chamber, the sun a bridegroom
That turned into a strongman in a stanza
Warming up as lightly as a dancer.
His race is on an ancient way-marked path,
His going forth is from the end of heaven,
His circuit's to its other end at last,
The topics of the old philosophers,
The statutes of the Lord, a little leaven
That we are lightened of as if by fears.

20 ❧ A Prayer for Iacopo
Of David

May someone
Or something
Hear you
When I'm not there,
Your heel against the wall,
And may that something
Set you high upon it,

The secret God of your old name:
May it spy you from its sacred home
    And seize you from its fall,
      Protect and lift you up.
           May it grant
           What you'll
           Have dared
           To wish
    According to your heart,
           And fulfill
           My gloved
        And outstretched art,
Which mimics words a king might chant.
      My heart's a lure
          That's swung
   To bring an ancient song
        Upon the ground,
        And from the sky
        To my right hand
        I mark it fly:
  A weight of wilderness,
          Which drops
         To hear
Fresh versions of a name's old sound.

21 ❧ Beechenhurst
Of David

      I want to make a poem
      Out of my earnest look,
   A photograph my father took
      Of me and my young mum
Under an oak at five a.m., my first
    Ever summer, Beechenhurst.

I have no memory of it,
There's no one else around,
I look like something that makes a sound
As soon as you shall sit,
My parents at rest, it seems, on the flight to Bream
Or Egypt, their dawn an Ancient's theme.

I found a rhyme and cried,
But three days later crossed
It out in scorn, which meant I'd lost
The heart of a stanza I'd
Had second thoughts about in any case
And left half-done in my sad haste.

But I digress: the poem
I want to make is of
A sword in my look, the kind of love
That waves you from your home
And severs piety, the love that joys
In your strength and takes you out to rejoice:

The love that is at odds
With what disturbs my art
And makes me hate those close to my heart
Who would prevent what's God's,
The face of them against my tempered glance,
Art's concentrated countenance.

22 ⚜ To Catch a Thief
Of David

I

You are so far from me, you cannot be,
As you are in that line,
The first thing on my mind,
And now I'm left alone, you let me see,
Your name's a door that someone double locked,
At which I hear no knock.

And yet I have a sneaking feeling that
              You're in this text, which cries
              Of yours have dramatized,
And in an upstairs room I'll find you sat,
As a thief inside a narthex craves perhaps
              The judge in the deep apse.

In light that comes to darken yet the night,
              I heard the tune for a Psalm
              They call 'The Deer of the Dawn':
It was a word that shone, but not to sight,
Stealthy as a thief in the night, for me
              To catch eternally.

II

That thing you've sought so very carefully,
              All your life
              Nine to five,
Reviling the cry when you have wondered how
I'll have material security,
              Is what prevents you now
              From finding God at home
              Or in this poem.

How could you give it up now that you're rearing
              A family?
              Earth's fatally
Ruined ecology cries in the daytime
And in the night season is in our hearing,
              But we're not listening, and I'm
              Among strong bulls of Bashan
              Besetting the Passion.

I tried my hand upon the door of the praises
              Of Israel,
              Of what is real
In its praise of God, and turned and met a thief
In the night of all things on earth whose race is

From the end of heaven: a leaf
To catch for luck from out
Our trembling doubt.

III

Drunk on wine, you covered me with your hand,
And passed me by.
As I awoke next day, I was told
My parents had unlaced my boots, and pulled
Them off, as I,
Uncovered and
Passed out, lay in my hall, or forgetful land.

These Psalms of mine have put me in a cleft
Of the rock to make
Me see I am that drunk on his farm:
The oblivious idealist that charms
The massing snake
Of tourists who drift
Like snow, whose form is in the eyes they lift.

I wondered if this poem is 'David's Complaint',
Or 'A Prophecy
Of Christ', the former a fourfold
Intensification of the latter's bold
Questioning cry,
Which grows more faint,
Before its words of praise for artist and saint.

However far I venture up this ladder,
Across this ceiling,
Backwards through this book, I should
Know over halfway through it is a wood
I have a feeling
Shall make me sadder,
No friend around, but drunkenness like an adder.

And yet there is a light I've seen in dreams
As if the bed's
Submerged treasure could catch the sun.
With lover and friend, all acquaintance, gone,
What is it sheds
Its light and gleams,
But what is made of what has passed it seems.

IV
The hearing of the Psalm
Was like a man
Who writes a jeremiad
Before the dawn
And finds beyond
The coldest whites
And greys and blues
Of its idealized
And half-imagined horizon
The lodging place
Of God: outlaw
Of the congregation's praise
Inhabiting now
The wasted words of my cries.

23 ﷼ A Stream Still Flows
Of David

I
Each season shares the adjacent seasons' weather
And summer wants no winter snows
To dream iconically, its sun a feather
Of colours found when whiteness slows
Or is dismembered

As it's remembered
In texts through which a stream still flows.

That stream restores its texts like spit on eyes
Of readers yet half-blind: I see
That men as trees are walking by the skies
Like driftwood forms the gods must free.
From out their mouths
A cutting sprouts
I might transplant eventually.

II

If they recite our common lullaby
The day they bury me,
It's only I shall miss the hoof-marked strips
Along the contours by
A wood upon a hill, how suddenly
They join into a dip,
Rise again,
And end below a tree, where sheep might lie
After they graze at dawn.

That pastoral song of spring falls on my mind
Like snow imagined in June:
My restlessness I find shall disappear,
The end of tracks that wind
Around the hillside's field, and now or soon,
Well-fed and free from fear,
No thought has swerved
From rod and staff, the kindly knife behind
The table at which I am served.

It is a song that's marked for evening prayer
Once a month, in the midst
Of life, not in the Burial of the Dead:
I hear it everywhere,
In the fields stretching to wastelands, and in the widths
Of sleep, like something read,

Or said aloud,
From off a stand before the starkest stare
Of a sad familiar crowd.

III

Because there was no room for them in the inn
She laid him in a shepherd's song
Whose secret theme she pondered in her heart
When through the door of the sheep they were gone.
It was a song as close to ancient signs
As any uncompromising lines.

This song it was that made
Her son an avatar:
Flesh reared to char, asleep in words
Her mother sang at her
Of acquiescence of a lamb that's blessed
By waters of quietness.

The lamb in the midst of the throne
That died upon the cross
Is the lamb that sings he's made to lie
In pastures of tender grass.
How many palms he leads of sons and daughters
To living fountains of waters.

I make these lines lead to an acquiescence
By phrases entered in my mind
I know not when like famous songs small children
Might just recall they sang behind
Mary and Joseph: angels with shepherds like lovers,
The innkeeper in tears when it's all over.

IV

The knife that's poised above
This line shall make
Its cup
Run over,

If not withheld, as in the silence of Isaac
In the presence of his father.

I do not want to be
Someone's idea
Of me
And find
My thoughts are like a sea of wheat in the sear
That waves into the wind.

The line that speaks these lines
Shall not falter
But winds
And rambles
Its way through off rhymes, prodded to the altar
I took to be a shambles.

V

The unconsuming flame that burns
No bush ablaze:
The fire that manifests itself
In speech that turns
Always
Itself
Away. The ground. The shepherd shoeless on't.
The Lord. My friend. I shall not want.

In homes of wolds of tender shoots
He makes me crawl and crouch:
Upon waters of quietness
He glints and leads me out.
The living breath along
My blood he turns about. He leads me on
The crooked paths hoofs make,
The track that must be right, for his name's sake.

Surely as I move inside a shadow
Of the valley of death I will revere
No evil: I shall not fear
Affliction with you
By me.
Your club and stick they make me breathe thickly.

Before
My eyes
You lay a board
Before my enemies.
With fat you fattened my head:
I was force-fed.
My cup
Fills up.

Ach, the beauty of *hesed*
Shall chase, put me to flight,
All the warm hours of my life,
And so I am arrested
In a world that is ablaze
The length of our hot days.

VI
Five times I've tried to make myself
Your lamb-like speaker, first,
Almost heedlessly, in June
I made you part of a burst
Of forty poems or so, and then it snowed,
Six months later, and I was awed

By your simplicity and strangeness,
Having been presented
With you in class the week before,
Not even when we'd ended
Our halting recitation of the whole
Recognizing you at all.

This second bout I've made four poems
And I am still too much
In a hurry, uninitiated,
Afraid almost of the touch
Of the shepherd, still too proud to wait and heed,
A child who wastes his courage on speed.

(That last line's lifted from a poem
I read the end of the day
I finished my last version of you,
A poem that would waylay
Its children, a poem I found that I was forming
Unintentionally that morning.)

VII

My poem burns with what it's not:
The Psalm that's placed upon its tongue,
As if it had a tongue to cry out at
The nothingness it feels between its sound
And what is being sung:
The theme it has found.

I am like a branded animal
Chosen for its sacrifice
And do not understand the hands that fall
Upon me by the table, their higher reason,
Which feels as sharp as ice
Inside its season.

'My cup runneth over' because
My lines contain, like no cup or cupboard,
That which contains. I follow them across
The line, a crooked route, and pant, or chant,
'The Lord is my shepherd,
I shall not want'.

Quotations of Places

Of David

I

Your margin's starred with texts dispersed
Throughout the rest of you,
Each text a universe,
If it's looked up,
Within whose skies or margins you're but
Another star or clue.

You are a line to take and wind
Around this world of ours,
The future sphere I find
In my blind hands,
Wrapped tight as rhyme that understands
The compass of the stars.

My life's an upturned etymon
That moves invisibly
By stars I see upon
Its complex roof
Or hull of sky: it is the root
Of a word that you'll supply.

A vessel changes in the space
Around our rooms of words
To bring its well-packed crates
In precious time
To ports of earth, to workers lined
In air so fresh it hurts.

I opened one ahead of time
And found your place of birth:
A nebula of rhyme
Or blank tirade
That went, where were you when I laid
The foundations of the earth.

II

The voice that lies in the gutter margin,
By the crowds, in the place of annotation,
This voice that's soon passed by and not looked up,
    That's bent into its shadowy station,
Doesn't beg for change, passed out in its socks,
    His place of defense the munitions of rocks.

Who'd ever want to wake him up?
You would not like his idiom among us.
I'd meditate the terror of his tongue
    And hear his stammering righteousness,
But I bet he's got the problems he warns me of,
    Would grab my newly dry-cleaned love.

III

For seven days I had too much out late
    The night before
To write, and then I came to the heads of your gates,
A man below the down-turned beaks of a door.

Today it feels absurd to say to them,
    Lift up your heads,
You gates and doors, and think that only then
The king comes in like something you must have read.

Who could this king of glory be today?
    No lord of hosts
That's crossed in battle: the little I can say
Is that he might be curled by the side of your posts.

25 ⁊ The Cat

Of David

I sit and wait, look blankly at my text,
   And think of a text to come.
      The fridge might hum,
But only a cat's imploring scratches vex,
    Upon the cellar door,
      The quietness
Of no one up as yet, its creak and snore.

Show me the way, I'll wait, I summarize,
    And want to copy out
      The text without
A change except slightly to modernize:
    Teach me your paths, O Lord,
      Show me your ways,
I write, switching, for quasi-rhymes, the words.

The cat is in the room at last and has
    Me bang about for food,
      Just as I would
Came there a cupboard sound of busy rats.
    My art is on all fours
      Inside a mass
Of words and waits at what it thinks are doors.

26 ⁊ One More Informal Anecdote

Of David

   Must I be subjected to
   One more informal anecdote?
      What should I do
      With someone's note
About a childhood spent in Ireland or Wales?
     Those stories' kind of morals?

I will not sit with such dissemblers,
Nor go in with a congregation:
I will remember
The habitation
Of your sound house, those lines where hands of sense
Are washed in innocence.

Gather me not with men of blood
Whose hands are full of mischief and bribes,
Verses of mud
And bits of lives:
My feet would climb upon a table land
Where I must take your hand.

Prove me and try my heart for size,
Teach my feelings what to say:
Before my eyes
I see your day
Of judgment rise inside my mind's confines
As I revise my lines.

27 ?᛫ *The Temple,* or *The Rock*
Of David

The city suffers from its homelessness:
The population of the world
Is on the streets and in a mess,
So wired on alcohol and spice, it's curled
Into a door,
Upon the floor
Like something dropped to be unfurled.

One thing it has desired that I will seek,
That it may dwell in your example:
To make your house again each week
And see your face inquiring in *The Temple,*
Reading *The Rock,*

Each holy book
That hides what it would most resemble.

What can that previous stanza possibly mean?
I see inside a room of words
A figure from the streets that leans
Into its book and murmurs, teach me, Lord,
Your way, and lead
Me where I read
The truth proceeds with flocks and herds.

28 ❧ Rock-Paper-Scissors
Of David

A page conceals a rock;
An open hand, two fingers cut,
But those, next round, the rock might blunt:
The unhewn block
Of which my writing's made.

It is the heart of a poem
About the impossibility,
Or high improbability,
Of making that poem,
No sound my words have made.

And many erudite,
Or wicked, people, in bars, or their books,
On Instagram, Twitter, and Facebook,
Draw me from it
With mischief in their hearts.

Hear my voice when I cry,
When I lift my hand, not in a round
Of scissors, paper, rock, but drowned
By that vast cry,
The oracle in my heart.

29 ≉ The Song of Solomon
Of David

You called to me, and called to me
(I thought it was about some chore):
You wanted me to see
A single fawn you saw
Through opened shutters, which paused and busily fed,
While you were putting our eldest son to bed.

The morning after I chanced upon
(As brambles ripened into August)
The Song of Solomon,
Opening the book that augurs,
While looking for this Psalm, behold! I read
How like a young hart at the window is my beloved.

The voice of my beloved! behold!
He makes the mountains to skip like a calf,
Upon the waters holds
The fire he cuts in half:
The voice of the Lord, behold, he makes the hinds
To calve, and takes the leaves that spring to mind.

30 ≉ 2 Kings 22
Of David

It was as if a book was found
And when I heard its words' admonishing sound
I took my laptop
And smashed it up,
And tore my file of work of ten years' past
To burn it with my precious pads of rough drafts.

The book was hiding in plain view,
And only rediscovered after you,

Or something, had
Me notice that
It kept on opening at a king's strong oaths
Who heard the book they'd found and rent his clothes.

It opened there each time I looked
To read this Psalm: something told me the book
The book had found
Was by the hand
Of David: something found each time the Temple's
Repaired, and what it signals, reassembled.

The Temple's site's the book and it's
Repaired and mended by the older poets.
What can I do
But write to you,
Untender as I am, and with my hands
At fresh cement project my pebbles of thanks.

31 ❧ The Summer Fly

Of David

Across these piles of pages
Lies work I can no longer stand,
Which once I thought so strong and so courageous:
The work I built on sand
Of thoughts too easily virtuous
When I was at my most industrious.

Let me not be ashamed:
I called and called, now bend an ear
Against my lines, and hear me cry your name.
I crawled upon the sheer
Face of your rock, to try and lay
Foundations there, and you brushed me away.

Pull me out of the net
Of these my complex lines, this tomb

Of lying vanities, and try to set
            My feet in a large room
      Inside your house upon the rock:
Behold, I lean against the door, and knock.

        Into your hands I commend
      My spirit with phrases broken off
A wavering song, which became a ghostly Amen,
          As if that were enough
      To enter the secret of your presence
Inside the book of the generations' lessons.

32 ≈ A Penitential Psalm
Of David

When first I tried to make your songs my own,
Without much knowledge, how your language works,
Or even how it sounds, spoken or sung,
Quickly I paged throughout concordances
And let mine eyes run under splendid entries
In massive dictionaries, down passages
Compiled so many centuries ago.
I thought your verses fructifying soil,
The passages at last a garden's paths,
And so I dug for primary roots of words,
But found my ignorant, literal style only covered
My sins in so much soil, and not at all
As God would, had I worked to lever them
Clean from out the cluttered ground. How hard
For a man to be righteous without his work. How hard
For me to say at last: 'Blessed is he
Whose transgression is forgiven, whose sin is covered.'

The Firmament

Of David

You said, he has the look of someone who's lived
Before, come back determined to improve.
I think he wails like the old imperative,
                    Sing a new song:
                    Our newest son,
As rough as a rock of Michelangelo's,
His larger self already on the move
From newly curling hair to curling toes.

His larger self's subtracted from the rock,
The newest heaven beaten out of earth,
As if we solved each statement's paradox
                    Each time we sang
                    The newest song
The oldest one would have us make again:
As if I'd heaped a sea of words at his birth
And beaten their matter to leaves of gold, or rain.

            In different kinds of situations
                Almost haphazardly
                    Over time
            A book was being handed to me:
        A book of books that must be added to
                To make it all come good and true.

            I've heard in ancient China each home
                Housed an anthology
                    Of poems to learn,
            To make one more eventually:
        Give me the skill to make one song for you,
                To bring from this book something new.

            The true Christian's the righteous man
                Who's trained his hand and tongue
                    To play to the Lord
            And sing unto him a new song:

Who lives by this command completes with his breath
The firmament that cracked at his death.

34 ✺ 1 Samuel 21–22

Of David

'Isn't this David king of the land?'
         He overheard
            Gath's servants speculate
                And frothed at the beard
And scrabled on the doors of the gate
         As if he'd lost his mind.

'And didn't the women sing of him,
One to another in dances, saying,
         Saul has slain his thousands,
          And David his ten thousands?'
             And what they said
             Made him afraid.

When he'd escaped to a cave, it's said
He made a song-preventing song
        To stop the songs he'd heard
          The women sang
          And have us instead
Magnify the Lord.

I praise all work that would divert
         An overflowing
          Of brash and knowing
Or boastful verse, to help convert
         Our brackish souls, and open
         The gates in us of heaven.

Who Is My Enemy?

Of David

Who is my enemy? All you
Who would frustrate me in this work,
Who would prevent its publication, review
It badly when it's done:
You know not what I'll do.

An ancient song has made you chaff
Wind blows, an angel chases you
Relentlessly along your slippery path
Of dark signification
Of signs that crowd to laugh;

Until the enemy's inside
Me too, which makes him nicely less
Forgivable, and now I see how I'd
Devour the Psalmist too,
His cries so magnified:

His Psalm's a hare, a tench, a wren,
My lines a greyhound, otter, merlin,
And finally a fine black-crested hen
To scratch the ground and swallow
The grain the song was then.

If I have swallowed up that grain
Let the grain be magnified
Into a boy, so I am not ashamed,
A child to cast to sea
To be reborn again.

I've seen and heard such dreadful things:
I know an old lady who swallowed a grain
And grew again to swallow the song she sings
And told a tale of lives
In oscillating rings.

What I perceive my problems are
I might just retroactively fix
And push them to their limits then, as far
As death, or Styx, or the lady
Beneath the blazing star.

36 ⁊ Lark in the Morning
Of David

Could I once see the world as yours,
And not a sump or mine,
Of oil and gold and metaphors,
Your qualities might shine
Up to the balanced clouds and cold ozone,
Its heaped-up plateau of bone.

For years I thought I was addressing
The sexiest of ladies
I would and wouldn't be undressing
Inside a grove of Hades:
My dream was such she was my world, a pool,
And I a groveling fool.

But now I see I was devising
Mischief upon my bed,
And strain to hear the lark that's rising
Into the things I've read,
The sound in light exhorting me to make
A new song for your sake.

The world's a man that was dismembered,
That lark's his fallen heart,
A future state that is remembered,
A faithfulness that's part
Of all I see or am, and holds, in fact,
The dream in which we act.

37 ⅋ Salt of the Earth
Of David

A crooked Z said to the upright A,
               Be kind to grass that's mown,
             See how it withers soon
        Exactly as you shall one day:
Why do you shun my earthly experience?
Sion, it's said, rose out of chaos once.

A song of wisdom children could recount
              Was set inside Christ's heart,
            Acrostically, to start
        The fire of his Sermon on the Mount:
Blessed are the meek for they shall inherit
The earth, he said, to found a house for the Spirit.

I know at first I was transplanted here
             To make a hiding-place
            Through which there peers a face.
       But since my canopy shall sear,
Archaically, at last, give me the art
To take what hides among my nests to heart.

38 ⅋ A Penitential Psalm
Of David

        Did he cry, Ai, las,
        The man that praised the lark
        Against the light, because
        He felt in love a dark
           Discrepancy
Like that between Lent's string of prayers
           And the infancy
Of spring for which the winter cares.

        His lady's stealthy absence
        Is God asleep in man,

Each dawn of ours the fragments
Of light before the sun
In Genesis.
Believe him when he says he'll die:
Such sicknesses
Manifest the oldest lie.

And do not flatter yourself
He led a life like yours
Of lazy affairs: your health
Disguises sinful sores
That man looks on;
He found himself a remedy
Of infinite song
And freed his wounds' old melody.

39 ❧ The Sojourner

Of David

I

I did not say, I'll stay in silence,
But I was silent night and day,
Like plates below an arc of islands,
My heart again will have its say.

But do not tell me too exactly
The measure of my days, the end
You have ordained for me so flatly,
My days are frail, their breadth an hand.

My lines are like a warehouse where
I worked, in hands of the receiver,
Man's life is but the building's air
We helped to raze the summer after.

What did I work for all those summers?
My hope was in the holidays.

You made me deaf and dumb and dumber,
Now hear my drowned volcanic cries.

II
I said, I haven't said it yet,
Not quite as I'd like to:
I'll have another go and take
Away a rhyme or two,
And give myself more space, look closely over
The original, then leave it altogether.

Like something from the Mabinogion:
You'd say, I'll grow up faster.
Wet sand mirrors a Michelangelo,
Your arm, an old prophet's musculature.
The hurried scribbles on my leaves, sublime
(Are something more substantial than my rhyme).

I lost my way through nights and hills
In boots and shoes and black tie.
I tore my back while heaping up
The treasure of the magpie.
But I was careless about my storing of it
And everything was scattered to no one's profit.

And when the season put on black
I sat around to wait
For your delayed delivery:
A long or dateless date,
Which took me from my work and leisure time
To nothing more substantial than a rhyme.

Give ear unto my cry and deaf tears
That they might hear the prayer;
A stranger, without, but like, his fathers,
Repeats phrases somewhere
Within my heart, to learn and speak his part:
The foreign language of the blood and heart.

40 ⅊ The Second Self
Of David

Isaiah and the Psalms, and not much else,
                                  Inside their mouth,
            The locals made a second self
                        Around the Sea
                        Of Galilee
That went and spoke as strangely further south.

These texts were planted in their upturned ears
                        And grew to be
            A final altar, hewn in tears,
                        The emblem of
                        The highest love
That said, I come: this book is written of me.

I waited, idly twisting sense, so I
                        Might make him squeeze
            My hand and bend an ear to my cry:
                        In wine's dark pit,
                        Or sea, he put
A new line to my mouth, of praise, like these.

41 ⅊ John 13:18
Of David

We sat and ate your bread, and then we eyed
                        Each other, stalled, amazed.
      His kick was an accomplishment of scripture
                        Against a state he'd rupture:
      His heels a hoof that quickly magnified
                        Itself into your face.

You knew all things were in his hands, that he
                        Came from and went to God.

I thought he went to buy things for our feast,
                    To feed the poor at least.
I couldn't comprehend, I didn't see,
                    How scripture there was shod.

That hoof has bruised these lines and kicked their sense
                    Mystically skyward.
What was it beguiled me when I did write,
                    That went out in the night?
I see betrayal of sense, fulfillment at once:
                    Unnumbered thoughts to us ward.

It's said one man's offence prepares us for
                    Another's righteousness.
I was beguiled and find I am betrayed
                    By everything I've made.
Each man's accomplishments slip out the door
                    And crave he'll rise to bless.

BOOK TWO

42   ## A Song inside the Night
The Sons of Korah I

You are my heart, the heart of everything
That's mine, the Word or world in which I move
                    And have my being,
                    My only love,
As certain also of your own have said:
The sad and potent offspring of the dead
                    That bring alive their
                    Legacies
                    Inside their river
                    Elegies:
The kind of things I used to think the highest art

When I would tread the rivers of their heart.

Deep calls to deep as on a shattered
Ledge behind a fall our roars
Are kept with all the weight of waters
Gone over them; as on the shore
Our voices out at sea are nothing
More than sound waves dreams prolong.
Each deep still calls unto another:
The sea inside a cave; a song
Inside the night; my thirst for what
It was that trod before the deer
That is not here, but in the quiet:
The living thing you make appear.
My tears are all the bread I see,
I lie like someone fast asleep
That bit upon infinity
Inside a brier no deer could leap.

43 ❧ Dear Inmost Soul
The Sons of Korah II

I'm at the end of a question asked
Right at the heart of your deep heart.
            'Why art
            Thou cast
Down, O my soul?' I ask, that I
Might climb, with someone else's harp,
The shaft of truths that lie
In light that's at the mouth of my heart.
How crouched you are to make your murmur,
        Dear inmost soul of mine:
Extend your hands a little further,
You just might touch a face divine.

44 ❧ Dear Friend

The Sons of Korah III

We have heard with our eyes, dear Friend, what work
You did in times of old, which one or two,
A few last higher minds, or blissful powers,
Heard with their ears, to write the stories down,
At one remove from wise illiterate nurses,
Or right in front of soft and sweet-voiced men
Whose leaky cottages they'd journeyed to,
The poorest vestiges of plots and structures
Grand and impalpable: the work you did
Back in their days of old. How you would drive
The nations out and plant them too, and break
And send them forth.

       Dear Friend of mine, command
Deliverances for Jacob, all the sons
Of Korah: the sad and potent river poets
That might let patience have her perfect work,
Fallen into diverse temptations, and then
Withdrawn from all the world, within a wood,
Whispering my middle name, in tears at night.
Through you we are a ram to butt and gore
Rustlers: your name will trample down intruders.
It's you who have delivered us, and put
To shame our shameful mockers, Friend, in whom
We shine, to whom we cast our praise. Selah.

Yet you, you have rejected us and cast
Us off like shoes you thought you liked the look of,
And bought and wore and found uncomfortable.
You do not fight our wars for us anymore,
You cause our armies to make their tactical
Retreats, and those that hate us live with us.
You rear us like a flock of lambs for Easter,

Taken from their ewes and ram to feed
A multitude of supermarket eaters.
You sell us for nothing, you make no profit,
A shepherd about to forfeit his flock and take
Another job first city he can find.
You make us an object of scorn for neighbours,
Something for them to look at lazily
While they must stand and smoke by their back door,
Something to mock for those that work around us.
You make us an extracted passage full
Of proverbs classes hate to write about
During half hour bite size examinations,
A bending of the head among the teens.

Is our heart locked up? Our feet have not
Turned back, though you have crushed us in a place
Of dragons, covered us in a shadow of death.
If we'd forgotten your name, dear Friend, or stretched
Out palms of hands to make of strangers gods
Would you not find this out? I thought
You lived nearby the secrets of the heart.
And yet for your dear sake we're counted as
The lambs that jump their way to make the shambles.
Awake, why do you sleep, my Friend? Arise
And do not cast us off, why do you hide
Your face and overlook our blank distress:
Our soul sinks down into the dust, our womb
Keeps close the earth, the whole of us embraced
In its inclusive grasp, a common pin
And tumbler lock two pins can figure out
When there's no key: arise, locate and set
Each at the lock's sheer line, love's tiny gap.

45 ❧ The Song of Unborn Singers

The Sons of Korah IV

My heart contains a voice
    Of many waters:
My tongue's a pen moved by
    Three ready writers.

I speak of light that would
    Be joined together
In holy matrimony
    As light and weather:

In clothes that drop with cassia
    And myrrh and ozone,
The sword upon his thigh
    The edge of dawn.

Ten thousand things make up
    A night of stories:
In gold of Ophir stands
    A cloud of glories.

Forget the lake and seas,
    Your mother's home:
The song of unborn singers
    Shall make your name.

46 ❧ The Stranger's Refuge

The Sons of Korah V

Soprano voices run toward a line
Of sheltering sound, as strong as stone in arcs,
Breathtaking like a hand just in the nick of time.

They teach us not to fear, although the heart
Of seas contains, at last, eternal creations
Of earth, and earth shakes badly in the dark.

Come, behold his works, what desolations
He makes of earth: he splits her like a shellfish
Into two parts at first, one half the stations

Of gods, fixing their stars, the other hellish
Earth, her neck the mountain pier, her eyes
The source of all great rivers that run their selfish

Course around a sea, her broken thighs,
The flooded deep. Be still, and know I am behind
Your eyes when you would build and realize

The stranger's refuge in our heart and mind.

47 ⁊ A Murmuring Song

The Sons of Korah VI

A cloud, or sphere of ether, fills with rain
            To empty on the earth: I know,
                        And don't know, how
            My clothes are drenched and dried again.
I see and do not see my sullen face
            In this sky's molten looking glass.

They start to clap: my praise, more circumspect,
            Still tries to figure you out. I strum
                        These lines and hum
            A murmuring song with little respect
For what is plucked: my heart makes lines, my mind
            Has cut, like tendrils purged of a vine.

Illuminated Manuscript

The Sons of Korah VII

A herd of cows among the sheep;
A ruined holy city heaped
      Below some hills and ashes:
The oaks and sycamores and brambles
Measured in minds of men that scrambled
      And died in hands of bushes.

A place of refuge in the north;
The heart of all that once poured forth
      Spontaneously from out
The sky, and when the strain was ended,
A place where time is still suspended
      Inside our trembling doubt.

Such are your places built by us:
Incomplete and ruinous,
      In words and broken stone,
Like wrecks of Tarshish beached in mud
Whose keels are spines the sea must flood
      Of men supine and prone.

Walk about this place, go round
About the squares and groves, and count
      Her unbuilt spires and towers:
Mark you well the mounds of bulwarks,
Her vanished roofs and palace walks,
      To make this book of hours.

Vain Trust

The Sons of Korah VIII

Two Christmases ago when I had tired
My rhymes to a kind of final red-eyed horror,

Trying to stay close to the letter
Of this Psalm of Korah
And a form of Mary Sidney's, I now see,
I couldn't say it any better:
'Worldly prosperity
Is not to be admired.'

I love these summaries, their quiet correction,
And running heads, inside the KJV,
Like lyric condensations in
The book of an LP,
Perverse tales paired down to 'Poor boy in ground',
'Drink blood like wine', 'Vain trust', and then
The Messianic sound
Of the word 'Resurrection'.

I'll not retain my first attempt to make
This Psalm again, but pray instead this hour
I'll 'build the faith of Resurrection,
Not on worldly power,
But on God', earnestly persuaded as
I am by this old song's inflections:
Its dark parable that's
More dear to me for thy sake.

50 ❧ Inside Our Common Eye
Asaph I

I

O God, God, God, the seed, the stem, the leaf,
The circle that dreamt of a circle, and drew itself apart
To make a portal, through which I see a thief.

The God of gods, my Lord, I find it hard
To name you: kindness, judgment, mercy, pry
Inside the flaws of my contracted heart.

You that live inside our common eye,
The line of all horizons in the mind,
As if there were a thing that sees up high:

Can it be that you have been so kind
As to have spoken to my unbelief?
Out of perfection of beauty they say you have shined.

II

The sun would be in someone else's hall,
Which then belongs to him, would dine alone,
And make himself a home away from home.

The earth's a tribesman host and says that all
That's his is mine. The sun has gone from court,
Shall not keep silence, fires consume his thought:

What does it mean that you recount my lines?
That you would lift my covenant in your mouth?
You that bear the word to make my house

Must taste my discipline: must be refined
Yourself, should you refine my lines and laws,
Should I recast a finite mind like yours.

51 🥀 A Penitential Psalm

Of David

The flower forgives the branch its falling short
Of March and would identify itself
With its ideal, the fruit it must have caught
Of air, another season's massive wealth:
Blot out those lines of mine that miss their mark
With flowers of loving kindness, flowers of March.

A multitude of words went out to me
And would be washed of business back in town.

Cleanse us, they said, of our iniquity,
Unloose us from desire as you stoop down.
Next day, as I was coming up for air,
A voice reminded me, I am your prayer.

Against you only have I sinned, you might
Be justified in saying (when you shall speak):
I was conceived in play and shaped in doubt,
But do you see I am the truth you seek,
The Russian doll that has no other in it,
The harsh note in the music of the linnet.

Cleanse me with hyssop: I shall find your voice.
Wash me and I am whiter than flowers of snow.
Play me back: my broken bones rejoice.
Blot out the iniquity of all I know.
Create in me a clean hospitable heart,
My lines shall sing as windows do in March.

52 ❧ 1 Samuel 21–22
Of David

When he was on the run from mad King Saul,
David lied to Ahimelech the priest,
And Doeg was there, saw David get the sword,
And later told the king, who called the priest,
     And slaughtered all his house.

But one of Ahimelech's sons escaped
And fled to David, and showed him Saul had killed
The priest, and David knew his tongue had shaped
That massacre: avowed his lies had filled
     The earth with all that house.

'Why boastest thou thyself in all this mischief?'
He might have asked of himself, that mighty man
Of whom the women sang, who sent to the chief
Musician this song, of Doeg they say, who ran
     His sword through all that house.

This song's two men in one, a tree that cries,
A sinner's final steps, the first of the saint:
It roots its maker from a land of lies,
And plucks you from your dwelling place, to plant
                    You by the river's house.

53 ⅙ The Chrysalis

Of David

                The earth's a spray of acrid leaves
        And men as larvae walk upon it far
                        From home, voraciously,
                        And guided mainly by fear.
            Their scheme of things, molecular,
                        They say that God is dead
            And eat this earth as we eat bread:
        Their mouths would alter irreversibly
                Our life-supporting atmosphere,
                            And then they leave
                            Soft forms well fed.

            O that they'd make a chrysalis
        To save themselves in death, so that the sky
                        Is made again a dome
                        Of golden bone on high.
            Or is it that this hot pigsty
                        We've made of earth, with all
            Our industry and vehicles,
        Is our chrysalis: a tomb or womb
                In which a Monarch butterfly
                            Is formed by bliss
                            Unutterable?

            The population of the world
        Commences hungrily its fifth instar
                        And eats its fourth cast skin.

I'd say it hasn't far
To go, at this late stage, before
It hangs itself down from
A leaf, to make its golden tomb:
Our leaves are all but gone by now, within
This abdomen and metaphor,
To be unfurled
When called upon.

1 Samuel 23
Of David

Arisen and departed from a town
He'd saved but didn't trust or know,
David and all his discontented men
Went whithersoever they could go
To evade King Saul (come out to seek his life)
And came to the wooded wilderness of Ziph.

It sounds in my ears a tale to tell my children,
A place their mind might just recall,
Of rocks of candy and rivers of babbling wine,
Except the Ziphims came to Saul
To give up David and make their wilderness
A name's dark home, a place where his haunt is.

What's in a name whose roots are in a wood,
A name that loosed itself at last
From nest and branches set into the sky
To fly beyond the words you cast
Or slang at it, as inconsumable
As that old bush from which I hear I am called.

A Jeremiad

Of David

I have seen violence
And strife in the city, mischief and sorrow
Asleep on its streets
As if there's no tomorrow.
And you, my pleasant friend,
I see you rush about, so full of care,
For me, or work, the rapid business
Of a kind of blind consensus I cannot share.

O that I had a voice
Uplifted to a wilderness
To sing these lines,
A voice that takes its rest
With all the climbers there,
To wake before the dawn, and make the trek
Upon the unpatrolled steep pass
To where they speak another dialect.

Who speaks these lines but me?
I see a seething pot whose face
Is Jeremiah's:
O for a lodging place
In some vast wilderness,
I hear it cry, stirred by the almond rod
Of a frowning boy, a year and a day,
Who licked three drops and spoke the word of God.

There's pain about my heart:
Anxiety's a hare, a tench,
A wren, inside
My guts, which chase and clench.
I see the earth without form
And void, no light in heaven: the mountains move,
The birds have fled. I hear the groans
Of a long labour, a grain in the hen or dove.

56 ❧ The Dove
Of David

The silent dove of distant places
Alights upon a mast,
Is swayed into the dawn upon
A melody we've lost:
The sight of her is like a fresh petition
Inside a song of commonplace expressions.

She is that song's unspoken word,
The gesture of assent,
Which makes assurances of faith
Of petition and complaint:
The consonant that went again and plucked
The flitting vowel in her imperial beak.

And if you send her out once more,
She'll only reappear
When there is no more sea at last
And doves are here and there:
It is the Spirit that moved upon the deep
That makes this window through which it might escape.

57 ❧ 1 Samuel 24
Of David

Inside the dark of the sides I stand,
Your ripped off skirt
A rag of cloth in my hand.
I've read your work
And see it is workshopped to bits:
In my path it was a pit
You'd dug and you had fallen in it.

Or is it that I grew with you
Inside this pit,
And when they pulled me through

Its brightly lit-
Up mouth, I saw it was, in fact,
A parable: our backs
To what's mysteriously exact.

And now I'm back I do not crave
What you bestow
On those inside the cave
Who note the show
Of shadows quickest: cave or pit
Or box, whatever it is
I'm in, O God, my heart is fixed.

58 ❧ Our Desert Ignorance
Of David

O how I'd like to take that phone
From your hands and smash it on the dome
Of your smart bone.
All those lies
That drown the wind's fresh voice
I'd break against its prophecy of ice.
Your lives are like the slime
Of snails silvering end rhymes.

But go ahead! Faster! And still
Faster! Someone will give you pills.
Earth must be filled.
Dams that are frozen,
Like stratospheric ozone,
Must be broken. Whoso cries 'Bote-swaine'
On a ship at sea shall rejoice
At the tempestuous noise.

Or is it that that book is yet
Unopened. Never mind. I bet
You haven't met
Your weekly target

Yet. Go on! The largest
War's ahead. And academic argots
Are soon learned to justify
The cause, or it deny.

I know an antic man who hid
His heart on feet he'd washed in blood.
His work's a seed
That still withstands
Our desert ignorance:
His head is rested on its paws, he takes no stance.
Through floods of ice and droughts
It flowers inside our doubt.

59 ❦ ## Where I Shall Wander
Of David

They grin and make a noise,
The twilit nest of evening, their childhood home,
And clutch their broken toys
While they receive their magic worm or bone.
Effably they talk on,
And belch, for who hears? Then wander up and down, or walk on.

They are zoomorphic forms
Shape-shifting quickly into one another
Or something strange that swarms
Across me, slapping my palms, my legion brother.
When they're not satisfied
They stay out half the night and get themselves quite fried.

These lines, so heedlessly
Conceived, are laboured over in the morning,
So I can hear, and see,
And feel, you are my strength, as they are forming:
They are the opposite,
So God is my defence, of what the others write.

60 ❧ Agony in the Garden

Of David

Not the one with the half-dead tree and vulture,
The cherubs brandishing the tools of the passion,
But the one that now hangs by its side
    With see-through toddler, chalice and paten:
      The biting cup of wine
        You'll not put down,
          Or drain.

The wife of Zebedee had wished her sons
Would drink that cup: two thieves were hanged instead
Upon Golgotha, the one that railed, the other
    That's now in paradise it's said.
      Why take that cup of wine
        Over so fine
          A line?

Cauldron or chalice, your heart's a book or grail
I'll open and drink of to the end, I thought,
As I stirred all year the frothing bitter broth,
    The herbs and things the woman brought,
      But then one day I tasted
        Your scalding *hesed*,
          This acid.

Awake, stand up, all you at the head of the street,
Who've drunk all night tumblers of astonishment,
Shots of fury in all the bars of the city:
    The wine inside these words is meant,
      Like hair of a dog, to take
        For kindness' sake
          Your headache.

61, 62, and 63 ❧ Crenellations

Of David

I

Some scholars say
It would be wrong
To overplay
The words, 'the end of the earth', and then prolong
The overwhelming of the heart
At this Psalm's start.
But I would overtake and bring
In fetters into it the King
Upon the plain,
And have his sons before him slain,
His eyes put out,
As at the end of Kings,
Or as it is played out in plot and subplot
Of a tragedy's playful transfigurings.
I've heard some say
They'd like to see
Me pushing further away
From my intractable
Original
Into unchartered territory:
The blacked-out space
Of man upon his perspectival race.
But I will claim
The heritage
Of those who fear your name,
Cornered in this late age,
The men stretched out
Inside a nook
Of blackened paradise: the open book
Downturned dove-like upon our cryptic doubt.

II

The rock that's higher than I could hope,
That turquoise arch
Above a king and patriarch,
Turns out to be
A golden concave step
To fold on fold of lapis lazuli.

The thoughts this work has caught and locked
Into exquisite
Figures on their postnatal visit
Are leaves in bud,
Which cure us of the rock,
If they'll pour out their heart along our blood.

III

In vivid sleep my soul's yours fully,
But then you rise and go
The length of China and Mexico,
Through Pisa, Delft, Caerphilly.
I follow, am detained, and cannot remember
My way back to the chamber.

The whole world is a tottering wall
My mind still runs along,
A loosely crenellated thing
We made of earth, our soul.
Early will I seek you, up from my bed,
When all is sung and said.

The Blind Process of Grace

Of David

I

I called some roofers up,
Hoping to get a quote.
They walked quite noisily above,
And bullied me, I thought,
Subtly with strong-armed words, to get work done
That day, right there and then.

Some time later it rained
And it was obvious
They hadn't fixed the leak that stained
My bedroom wall. I cursed
And called them up. They were quite vague. And then
I called another in.

He said they hadn't done,
It seemed, a thing up there,
And that, in his humble opinion,
They'd stitched me up. I stared
At him, incredulous and disillusioned,
Still hoping for a solution.

He said he'll come again
And see what he can do.
Meanwhile I patch this poor complaint,
Reflashing it for you,
Or so my voice can lie inside it, dry
By night, preserved up high.

II

During this time of lightning missives
And information massed
As quickly as
The Capitol was once exhaled in Hell,
That fabric massive
Upon the smoking hill;

During this time of cities at
    A fingertip's disposal,
        Their business and bustle
Something to visit or puff at until
        They're lying flat
    And we're all dead or ill:

During this time we can of course
    Hope for the undeserved
        Grace of the Word.
Or is it that what heard our prayer trips round
        Us now, his course
    The soundproof veins he found?

The inward thought of every one
    Of us is deep enough
        For what's above
To move upon so it can take our face
        And sing our song
    Of the blind process of grace.

III

It is a text that shall require
The child who knows and smiles at God,
Who's wrapped inside a leather bag
And cast to sea by some old hag:
        'All men shall fear
And shall declare the work of God.'

The strength in which God shoots and is green
Is the strength in which his son is born:
The child I found when I had turned
Away from expectation, spurned,
        No longer keen
To find employment, and quite forlorn.

Give me the strength to build a house
So I can rear this babbling child,
I want to ask, although I know
Not even God himself can go
                        Inside this house
I want, that I myself must build.

65 ⁂ ## Above Allusion
Of David

I
                        Here it is, the song
That gave its purse and half an arm and shoulder
                        To go upwards along
A path of coldest oxygen and dust.
                        It is a song much older
Than that which speaks and leads and casts his eye
                        Upon a boat or buoy
And those far off whose tracks his sight adjusts.
                        This song bestows a jewel
And makes its prayer as flesh that can't withstand,
                        Quite happily, this cruel
Enacting of its death and preservation.

II
                        A father takes the hand
Of his poor son, his sight concealed as clouds
                        Fill up wheel ruts, and clods
Reflect with pools and crops sky's elevation.
                        I do remember now,
The strength that stills the noise of seas and men
                        Has made his sword a plough,
His chariot the glint of a farmer's tracks,
                        His oar a winnowing fan:

The hand once stretched in its abundant rage
                              Now sweeps across the page
Soft words a savage race forgets it lacks.

The Heart Is Made of Earth
Of David

                              Make a noise and split
The earth that's standing by to cover you
                              With earth, the book of books
You're buried in and are committed to,
                              You pastures wrapped in flocks,
                              You valleys shrouded in wheat.

                              All the earth's dug deep
Into its consciousness, like bulbs in spring
                              About to face what's raised
Over the top, like songs we needs must sing,
                              Imagination's raked
                              Back in the earth it leaped.

                              In misery I am earth
I heard it said, as I was carried out
                              By friends already dead
And soon to be quite drunk: I cried with my mouth,
                              I see it must be said,
                              The heart is made of earth.

Let the People Praise You, O God
Of David

                              The ends of the earth are skeptical
Of lines beginning with the word God,
                              O how they'd hate to see an O,
Or anything so bloody rhetorical.

In fact, they'd rather go
Out shopping or clubbing, maybe get some food,
    Than read a poem at all.

Or maybe they're packed inside a ship
That moves into the dark and find they have
    To pray to something, their prayers beginning
With God or O, the ship abandoned to slip
    Beneath the rainbows thinning
Upon the swell, a kind of face in love
    That dies with praise on its lip.

Let the people praise you, O God,
Let all the people praise you, someone sings
    At the top of a house, two hours a day,
A self-regarding, sweet enough, old sod,
    Who doesn't seem to pray,
Or sing: his praise adjusting words and things
    That sleep upright and nod.

68 ❧ No Return to the Land of Youth
Of David

I

Whatever it is that rides upon
    The heavens of heaven stoops from
His saddle, seizes with one hand
    A rock we struggled with,
        To hurl it
Somewhere for us in our familiar land.

II

Lightened in that instant I found
    Myself stunned on the ground,
Struck from a land that melts as God

Before the fire of reason,
A cloud
Whose strength is in the skies of our roughest season.

III
The god who is a father of
The fatherless, who wounds
Your hairy scalp in fiery love,
Picks himself off the ground
And looks
With eyes of earth at hands like hills that shook.

He sits hemmed in with greenwood trees,
In his ears a blackbird sings,
Like lines of marginalia coiled
Into a Psalm's gold wings:
The spoil,
Which women divided, from vanquished enemies.

69 ❦ Hygieia
Of David

The day I open your book
In an acceptable time
And heal the broken hearted,
Recover sight to the blind,
Is the day I'll hear them ask,
Is this not David's son?
Physician heal yourself,
They'll say, since I'll have come
Back home and squared up to
My mother, taunted my
Poor sister, so they'll say,
Offended by my dry
And weary cry. Meanwhile

I am sunk in the depths
Of mire and marvel at
Their unbelief: three steps,
My toes are in deep water.
You know my evil nature,
My sins cannot be hid,
I am merely your creature:
Dark waters flood my heart
And lungs and head. I sit
In the gate and make you the song
Of a drunk that lost his wit.

I thirst. My ears shall tingle. That's it.
A hand upon a wheel has marred a vessel,
And folds the clay
Of my last cry,
Returns and makes again another bottle,
Which seems as good as he can make it.

That bottle's baked by your opinion
Of it, and I shall get that meaning, take
It to the gate,
Teach you your fate:
These things you think are nouns are hands that break
These streets to make them their dominion.

Beyond our common wall, inside
Her terraced house, a bright-eyed woman lets
A serpent sip
From out a cup
She holds: against that wall my hands are pressed,
I bow myself with all my might,

And praise the tiny ash, the seed
That makes and magnifies the pavement's cracks:
The rod or branch
That takes its chance
Out of his root, its leaves so many flags
Of propagation, things to read.

Wolves A-Howling

Of David

I'd like to set you to
The tune
Of 'Wolves A-Howling',
So you can make no tarrying,
And hurry
Out across
The peaks of wild Arkansas,
The heights of south Missouri:
Make haste, O Lord, to help me,
Make haste, O God, to seize me,
Can't you see the wolves a-howling
All round my pretty little darling?
The tail end of
Another text,
The prelude to
The song that's next,
This song is but an interlude
Of perfect prayer
With hardly any words
That fiddlers howl with care.
And I would put it in
Some wild quatrains
To try and heed
The Word that frames
Its words:
Make haste,
Let them be confused
That chase
My living soul,
That howl
And are a-howling
All round my darling.
Let all that seek you
Exult and howl,

Let God be magnified
Inside my soul.
As I am poor and needy
Make haste to seize me:
O how the wolves are howling
All around my poor little darling.

71 ❧ David of the White Rock

I

Because they're brought by night to silence,
I've climbed up Pen y Fan and Scafell Pike,
The high places, to weep, and there I sense
The Forest howls all round them like
A shape around mined scowles:
Through streets of its towns everyone shall howl.

Among these fugitives that flee,
At last, my heart cries out for David, leant
Upon his harp, one time, eternally,
In someone else's poem, that's meant
For no one's ears but mine,
His hands lifted to play his yarns of the line.

Quicken me from depths of earth:
Be my outcrop, my castle at its top,
Once ruinous, as at the time of birth
You took me from the womb, and dropped
Me gently on the scales,
And brought me up half in and out of Wales.

Now I am at the screes of age,
My hair grizzled at the back, let my mouth
Be filled with praise. My words upon the page,
Like monstrous works published in youth,
Unperturbed by doubt,
Are things that howl I cannot quite blot out.

That poem about the rider left behind,
Fallen from his horse into old age,
        That one about a blind
Old man (another one) who fell on stage
In someone else's play and gave me eyes,
        That one in which I gave
      Myself a voice from out the grave,
These poems of mine I cannot quite revise:

They are opaque to me as the December
I wrote them in, as full of holes, in truth,
        As nights I half-remember,
And yet in this equivalent of Ruth
And Exodus, this book of lamentations,
        They have their place, and things
      Shall only get darker, I think,
In the next book, which floods my ruminations.

The Book of Psalms is structured like a cave
In which I am pushed for my initiation:
        The bedded rocks that pave
My way tip me to chaos of creation
Until I am substantially submerged
        And my head's a dove that broods
      Between the roof and the floor's floods,
A sphere that moves upon them as if it's urged.

72 ❧ The Climbing of Snowdon

I
Since they were poor and benefited from
        His magnanimity,
That King that made his large and cedar room
        Inside their crimson soul,

They made new songs to praise him endlessly,
        Prayers to open the scroll.

I saw some said, he shall come down like rain
        Upon mown grass, another
Thought he soaks a fleece of wool, the same
        Text in different mouths,
Like earth around soaked seeds, the jealous brother
        To hordes of threadbare sprouts.

They heard it said, the mountains shall bring them peace,
        A heap of corn at their top,
And thought that in the future stalks of wheat
        Shall grow up to the sky's
Harvesting height, the grain like fruit undropped,
        A cow's kidneys in size.

I read the text and get my parables
        Reversed, or find I think
Of someone turned about through mist, which pulls
        No shale, but mountain turf
And moonlit boots, the peace that's there on the brink
        Of what can pull such surf.

II
        The reading of the book,
        Accomplished in the making of
A book, is my initiation: one book
        A tunnel down
        Into the ground
Of the other, where like a dove
A voice brings forth her firstborn son to bless
        My anguished consciousness.

        One book is made in the other's
        Image: it is a child that would
Identify one day with things his mother's
        Pondered in
        That heart, within

Her heart, that's dark as any wood
Of fairy tale, the better for her to see
Potentiality.

(The Space between)

72 and 73 &

I found you out by chance,
Performing a sort of sortes:
Two pages opened out,
  You took by force
My thoughts and settled in doubt,
  No doubt to build
A new high house of prayer and chants.

How to divine that space,
The pages opened at,
Between two books inside
  A book, and that
Itself a book inside
  A larger book:
A threshold that was Janus-faced.

I looked before to rain
Upon mown grass, to crops
That wave their fruit upon
  The mountain tops,
And found a prayer for a son
  To save the poor,
And a moon that endures as a glorious name.

I looked after, tried to
Reverse the order of what
I thought I'd chanced upon,
  But found my feet
And steps were almost gone
  Chasing a tongue
That runs through the house on its hard shoe.

BOOK THREE

73 ⅜ Into My Dark Imagining

Asaph II

When you arrived last night I wasn't dressed
As yet, still going round to make and air
These empty rooms for my expensive guest,
And now their hangings are, first light, threadbare.
My feet had almost slipped, my steps at best
Were tentative, upon the dusty stair,
Trying to fix a golden antique structure
Upon my creaking house: the whole of scripture
Upon my lines just like a circle on
A square before the invention of the squinch.
In a doorway your feet were well-nigh gone:
My house was broken up. You came to pinch

My things, I think, your face a torch that shone
Into my dark imagining each inch
Of this my house is grander than it is:
A foot at least of scrolls and grotesque motifs.
The cynosure, on his progression, wakes,
As from a dream of instantaneous
Man-made destruction, finds his head now aches,
And that he hates his host's prodigious house:
The fireworks lit for him beyond the lakes,
The Doric paneling and its brisk mouse.
His heart is sore, his kidneys pricked with what
They poured last night in hall and high banqueting hut.

74 ⅜ All Naves

Asaph III

All naves were once an open ringing place
Of quick percussion tools: the pick, the wedge,

The many chisels making at the edge
Of local stone a king or monkey's face.
But then the hammers touched, in other hands,
Not chisels, but the heads of beautiful
And holy women found once not quite still
In stone and smiling under headdress bands.
The fires of Hell were whitewashed out of mind,
And now we see no signs, no saint among
The windows tells us anymore how long
Before you lift your feet, pluck out your hand.

You that moved upon the face of the deep,
That had us once translate the whole of scripture
Into chaos of centuries of secular literature,
You're now a poor man's turtle dove asleep
Upon the snake that coils inside my wrist,
Its many heads inside my right hand's fingertips.
Can you be stirred by songs that move my lips,
The deepest matter that comes as if to be kissed?
The day is yours. The night also is yours.
You broke the heads of dragons in the waters,
But then we broke the heads of all Eve's daughters.
Rise up along my mind and plead your cause.

75 ❦ Say, It Is Not So
Asaph IV

We're all a stage, not theatre, audience,
And rarely understand the private nature
Of public words, their special prescience,
Unsure if it's God that speaks the speech, or his creature.
And did he have, if God it was that spoke,
A Psalm in mind about life's wine, the dregs
This vault brags of, whereof the ungodly suck,
That time he swore his hasty love was vexed.

And as for me, I interrupt the speech
Some say is God's, to say, I'll speak to God,
But find my words are horns sawn off, that reached
The sky, that someone else must blow, or drink of.

76 ⫚ Vow, and Pay
Asaph V

They published eighteen of these Psalms of mine.
I talked about the making of the book,
This larger book, and they all sounded fine,
My poems on air that afternoon. I took
A call or two and ordered food online.
We drank prosecco, ate some cheese, and looked
At messages posted on Facebook. 'Thou',
However, 'art more glorious and ex-
Cellent', pushing my wine upon my lap-
Top, tantrumming 'when thou art angry'. Now,
Like then, scarcely appeased: a fist that wrecks
My sticky keys, the child of a mishap.

77 ⫚ The Cave
Asaph VI

A voice that rarely went to school now keeps me up,
Is pleasured to cry incessantly above my bed:
Insatiable and crazed by drugs, a thief on top,
This voice possesses me, and all I've known and read.
It is a strip of tapestry I made of balls
Of yarns, and days and years, my foreground figures stressed
Against abruptly vanishing orthogonals,
My mind a cave of urns of bees and beams of webs.

Your way was in the sea, your feet upon the wave:
The waters saw and were afraid, were spread apart.
But now the waters run as tears throughout this cave:
Call to mind your song in the night, look in my heart.

> But wait, I left the middle out, forgot
> The final lines, the questioning and praise,
> The hand of Moses, the people like a flock,
> So charmed was I by your mysterious ways.
> Have you, our father, cast us off forever?
> Are we forgotten? Is the promise barren?
> Your right hand's years I said I will remember,
> And take again the hand of Moses and of Aaron.
> Who do you say I am? The father, not
> The son, still asks, the eternal question posed
> By consciousness to us, his partial lot,
> Supposer still as well as thing supposed.

78 ❧ ## The Lost Ballad
Asaph VII

I made a ballad out of you, the first
Time round, in emulation of the poems
Of Christopher Smart, whose blazing song-like burst
I love the most of all our Books of Psalms.
I do not like most of my ballad now,
And have consigned it to a document's
Oblivion, so I may wonder how
I may again rehearse, or make some sense,
Of sentences in your hard parable:
'The heav'ns exterior doors' you handled 'with
Munificence and thrift' of David's rule,
'For children yet unborn', the creaking myth.

Ruination

Asaph VIII

I'll tell a parable I read somewhere,
Of someone's palace found in disarray,
An upturned table by a splintered chair,
The gorgeous poles and hangings stripped away,
Its marble floors a filthy lake's hard bed:
A chance intruder thinks the place abandoned,
A more perceptive reader sees a sanctioned
Hand at work, as if the chaos said,
Spring-cleaning has begun; no object's to be
Untouched now that the building's disassembled.
A sage likewise rejoiced to see the temple:
A fox that sniffed the heaps prophetically.

They laid Jerusalem on heaps, dissolved
In air a thousand abbeys once upon
A time, the dates of their destruction shelved
In books another age might chance upon
To find its new source texts, or fresh resolve
To build long after the second temple's gone.
I dreamt my family hunted the forest boar
And vivid grotesque animals from old
Church walls, zoomorphic forms and fabled beasts
Upon the primrose-spotted hill, before
The coppiced wood: they tasted like a tale told
Of flesh of saints in mouths of bird and beast.

Help us someone to cover our mistakes
In bitumen, and purge away our sins.
Of flesh of saints of earth our mouth still tastes:
Detox us of grotesque imaginings.
Why should the cities ask, where is our God?
Let him be known among the populations.
What manner of stones, what kind of elevations
Do you see here? What pavements have you trod?
There shall not be one stone upon another

That shall not be thrown down as I am raised.
I am the sighing prisoner, your lover:
Let my sighing change in folds of praise.

The True Vine
Asaph IX

They say an imitation should be as
A son is to the model of his father.
My imitations are unruly as
My sons: they test the patience of their father,
Require a lot of clearing up, and smile
My grandad's smile when they're brought down at dawn.
I have nourished and brought up children while
They have rebelled against me: children gone
Away backward with alienated features.
As buds in March shine out of stems, or earth
The sun's osmoted, I am a promise of creatures,
And something like creation marks each birth.

The vine that twines itself about old pages
In coils of parables and prophecy,
Its roots in harvest songs recalled by sages:
That vine they were, this vine I am, I see
It overgrowing still my forms and strictures,
Requiring sharpened moods of higher reason:
The ear that knows the soundness of a line,
Before it even knows I am the vine,
That purges slips it cut from Holy Scripture
Across a pattern season after season:
The awareness of bliss in sound, of being born,
Out of which leaves and fruit pass into form.

You brought a vine from Egypt, planted it here,
It took deep root and shadowed its room of land
With outstretched cedar arms and god-like hand:

She sent her shoots to sea, her branches the Otter,
Derwent and Ister, Thames and dark Swatara,
But now the boar wastes them, each hungry wayfarer.
A spirit rests upon a branch, and moves upon
A sea of all those rivers, men in shoes
Upon them, travelling down those highways, loose
Upon the waves like migrant workers gone
Forever, forced to live in a salt land,
Their hearts deceitful so none can understand.

81 ❧ 'And you shall love'
Asaph X

'Take a Psalm and make it sound again
And blow the heart's ram's horn each equinox.'
I failed before, I'll try and fail again,
To speak this Psalm as if I had God's voice:
'I eased his palm and shoulder from the hod.
From the straits you called, I pulled you out.
I eyed and answered you from where I hid,
Under the cover of thunder I heard you shout.
I tested you beside the waters of strife:
Open your mouth wide and I will fill it.'
He should have fed them also finest wheat.
'With honey from the rock I gave you life.'

'Hear, O my people.' There's a phrase occurs
Just twice in all the books of older scripture:
And you shall love, a phrase to put on doors
And gates, around the hearth and fireplace, to picture
Inside your heart-shaped heart. And you shall love
The Lord your God with all your heart and soul,
With all your mind and strength; and you shall love
Your neighbour as yourself: each phrase the whole
Of the other once they're understood together,

Their separated twofold rarity,
In sacred exegesis of the lover,
Giving them now profuse profundity.

'I tested you against the place of strife.'
I struck the rock of all I thought there is.
'From thirst of literal truth the spring of life
Springs forth.' The germ of truth is water's bliss.
'Live your life according to the truth
You have discovered: draw from pots of stone
Their water turned to wine: the only proof
You need is felt along your marrowbone.
Open wide your mouth and I will pour:
I am the consciousness that makes these lines,
Someone must have published, the opened door,
Or pierced side, letting out the water's wine.'

82 ❧ The Feast of the Gods
Asaph XI

God stoops among the gods and shall disturb
Their languid feast just like Silenus' ass.
A wakeful Mercury, still unperturbed,
Looks on as sleeping Lotis is caressed:
A pair of recreated river Gods,
Their mirrored poses make Priapus God.
I take the ass to be translated man
That has prepared himself unwittingly
To be before the obscured wood the one
That makes the Mystical Nativity.
The girl that balances the pot of wine
Is balanced by a faun's fake porcelain.

Silenus' ass lets out his newborn's roar
As red Priapus stoops to make his move.
Although they do not know it yet, what pours

Its indignation out and stamps its hooves
At this drunk act, among these drowsy gods,
Is not just Silenus' ass, but half our God,
The guard and glory of the garden plot,
Their mind, now waking up, that they forgot,
Which says, 'How long will you unjustly prove
The wicked just? Selah. Defend the poor:
They walk in darkness, earth's foundations moved.
I said you are gods, I show you now death's door.'

83 ⁊ 'I cannot bring myself'

83 ⁊ **'I cannot bring myself'**
Asaph XII

I cannot bring myself to change the poem
To come, or highlight it and copy, cut
And paste. I've read it through and now it's going
To have to stay put, all the faults I shut
Inside it mostly still intact. But then
Again, I write this retroactive fix,
Rereading obstinate lines, and they are men
Confounded under Sisera at the brook of Styx.
Make them like a wheel, like chaff in storms,
These lines that still must chatter in the choir.
These piles of words I lit with ideal fire
Are but old names consumed to common forms.

Let them be quiet and see our Hercules,
The bright-eyed man that died and was a god,
To whom we say, O God, hold not your peace,
Keep not your silence, be not still, O God.
When he is angry and kills, takes pity and heals,
It's not that some are killed and others saved,
But one man's state of mind's the battlefield
When God becomes the storm upon the waves.
Those thoughts that talk and cannot hear the choir,

Make them like a wheel, as chaff in storms:
Relight your pile of days with ideal fire
To burn exotic names to common forms.

The Swallow

The Sons of Korah IX

What forms I see my longing takes
        And turns them slightly round
           As if to see
           That there might be
      Another side or sound
To flesh that cries, a heart that aches,
My soul that faints for all your sakes.

Yea the sparrow has found a nest,
        Upon a chancel's shaft,
           The swallow her house,
           Now ruinous,
      Against a ruin's half-
Eroded voussoirs: something to test
And make again, to brood and rest.

Prosperous the man, and blessed, whose strength
        Is at the lightest edge
           Of longing night,
           Whose heart's the site
      Of dawn's transparent ledge:
Two circles separate the length
Of one that goes from strength to strength.

That man's a beak-head portal, a word
        Of ours opens and shuts:
           A valley of tears
           That disappears
      Along its rain-filled ruts.

O Lord of hosts, will you have heard
His prayer that folds with flocks of birds?

An hour spent under golden stars
    Of liernes is better than
        A thousand days
        Inside a maze
    Of boardrooms: their shapes span
A New Jerusalem of ours
That's built and wrecked every few years.

85 ❧ Early Flowers
The Sons of Korah X

    You that made us, you that freed us,
    Once or twice, a thousand times,
    Determined as we are to test
    The hidden law of obvious rhymes;
You that grew to be a man and said,
    It is expedient I die:
        Where is the Spirit you sent?
    The quickest truth in your darkest lie.

    And how could you become the world
    That hated you? A thing asleep?
    So small it cannot smile as yet
    Or roll itself upon the deep.
In each of us that came to hate you,
    Mercy and truth are met together:
        A nose touches a cheek,
    Ripeness and peace have kissed each other.

    As gaudy shapes of early flowers,
    The spirit of truth shall spring from earth:
    Ripeness breathes upon the sill,

And stays the weeks after the birth.
Yea that form shall grow and spread in beauty:
The earth shall move inside what's sweet,
Shall come again to us,
And set us right upon our feet.

86 ॐ In Fear and Trembling
Of David

Who bends his ear to hear me?
So very close
As I am poor and needy.
A dancer on archaic prose
Preserves my soul and makes me holy
As I tread on his toes daily.

Or is it that I crawl
Through roots, then stone,
To his original
Arrangement of words, and find, alone,
The God of gods, against a vein,
Repeating in verse his name.

In fear and trembling I turn
The finished page
Upside down: winters burn
Their limestone skies, as from a cage
Of opened twigs, and what were roots
Are beam-transfiguring shoots.

Teach me the path: unite
And knit my heart
To that which lies inside it,
So I may stand and then depart,
My hand upon the lichen clothes
Of a figure hiding in prose.

87 ⁊ This City
The Sons of Korah XI

The primal distant mountain
That looms from out the plain,
From out our hills and mountains
As crown of a cosmic chain
Of rocks of mountains, is his foundation:
The base of a city of gates of nations.

I will remember Rahab
And talk of Babylon,
America and China
Shall know Svalbard and Cape Horn:
This man was born and brought up here,
That man was brought up and born there.

Or so I've heard it's written,
The highest counts them up,
In the register of peoples,
This city of works of love.
The singers, musicians, and dancers, sing,
'This City of Love' and 'All My Springs'.

88 ⁊ Affliction
The Sons of Korah XII

They say they want a sincere heart:
        A broken form that wails.
But what of the units of heaviness
        Below the darkest details?
The world itself oppresses me,
        I'm free among the dead:
Anxiety itself is anxious,
        I cannot look ahead.

Hungover philosophy is sprawling,
    Draws near unto the grave:
Familiar metaphysical locution
    Is afflicted with your waves.
Lover and friend and family
    Have all fallen apart.
I cannot see the essential pole
    From this substantial dark.

89 ❧ Tondo

I

Not only your arms but also your infant Christs
    Have a kind
Of horizontal verticality
    That writhes around, wriggles behind,
    Reality:
    On knees of Neoplatonists
    Something that tests solidity.

Face turned away, his arms are stretched out still
    In one tondo:
Posed as something purposefully spilt;
    His mother's face is tending to shadow,
    Like columns split
    Into corners of a vestibule
    When a giant pulled it inside out.

The barely containable solidity
    Of a two-year-old,
Like an arm out of the Psalms, or from the ground
    When everyone at last is called,
    Expresses the round
    Of our lives in its entirety,
    Our being bound and again unbound.

II

This poem cannot be
An excuse for it. My *Book of Psalms*
Has been revised, and yet again
Revised, until I see
I'm making no improvements. Despite my qualms
I'll stop. My lines are now a source of pain,

And comfort too, at times,
No tinkering of mine can mend,
And every retroactive fix,
Each verse I add that chimes
The time of another's faults, would just extend
A book already longer than most would risk.

I'll have to let it go,
Like a son at school, and turn away
To get on with some other task,
While others coax and goad
Some meaning out of what it seems to say,
And trust it can rise to most of what they ask.

There is no image for
This other task imprinted on
My soul inside the middle of
The Psalms, where you bring forth,
For each intrepid reader, your firstborn son,
But I will keep at it, like a man in love.

III

I came upon the Book
Of Psalms' doxologies
Lying together in a nook
Of vanished paradise like old felled trees.
Blessed be the Lord, they might have said,
From everlasting
To everlasting,

This filled up earth their bed.
Such wondrous things,
They must have been, to make us sing,
Amen and amen,
Again and again.
Struck with their chords,
It might have been that everything
That hath breath praised the Lord,
Or so they hoped we'd sing.
But they were lying like a crown cast off,
Beside a hedge, before the building of
A new estate, without their Psalms,
The remnant of a hilltop farm.

BOOK FOUR

90 ❧ Someone Else's Epigraph

You caught my eye when you were just
Someone else's epigraph;
I wanted you to be my own,
To fall into my arms and laugh
At little things I would observe or try:
I copied you out so in love was I.

Your repetitions at the end
Almost made me cry that time,
And some time later, taking stock
Of what I thought I had of mine,
I found you out by a kind of providence
Opening a book inside a book by chance.

I loved your vulnerability,
Your ancientness, the kind of prayer
You made, its delicate insistence
That just might change the listening air:

Establish it for us, the work of our hands,
Establish it, the work your hand commands.

And let its beauty be upon us:
Let your work be shown to children.
Make us glad as many days,
And years, affliction has bewildered.
And satisfy us early with your song:
Change your mind, loved one, return. How long?

91 ☙ Is God among Us Here, or Not?

Is God among us here, or not?
That question steps before me like a witch
Dressed in feathers, pushing a pram
Towards a bridge,
Then floats with other feathers on my thought,
As I reread this Psalm.

A child murmurs above my head
And I can tell he's suffering in his sleep.
He woke me earlier with slight
Sad cries for help
And then went back to sleep, his nighttime dread
A letter like moonlight

Disturbing slant identities
Of sound between components at our ends
As it is sent from room to room.
Something bends
To words I want to say to this disease
That walks about our home:

It shall entwine you in its feathers
And snatch you from the snares of fowlers, from
The heavy breath of speech that tempts.
It stoops upon
The words that make these lines like light in weather
Unpitching fast its tents.

92 ⅋ The Gourd

The work this poem celebrates
Makes my couch a shady space
Below a summer sycamore.
It's only March, an hour before
The dawn, but this old Sabbath Psalm
Has made my living room a palm,
Or heavy tamarind at noon,
These lines of mine, which I should prune,
A half-exotic espalier,
A tree that was transplanted here,
And somehow trained on either side
My window frame. Although I've tried
To tie it fast, this sudden gourd
Is but a lesson from the Lord,
Which flourishes and withers just
As soon, if I refuse to trust
The meaning gathered in its leaves.
It is a chorus that deceives
Me into thinking that it's spring
Outside and everything must sing
As yet behind the leaves to come
Without sight, nothing deaf or dumb.

93 ⅋ The Reservoir

This poem floods around a song, until
             Someone somewhere sees
No pinnacles upon its crenellations,
             No twigs of canopies
Around its cockerel's golden comb, which I'll
             Have dropped in decreation

Without decreasing circles being made.
             The song's inhabitants,

Time out of mind, are fish, and I shall lie
On cold significance,
Which swells above, until I find I'm laid
On a coral tower to dry.

94 * A Dialogue of Self and Psalm

I

Self. Observe this Psalm's lesson, you burnt-out beasts
Of burden, who make up this late
World's booming population: you obese
Halfwit automatons, who ate
This world for breakfast, when will you sit up
And stand and walk and look around?
When shall your eyes see shapes you found
In your last death before you drained the cup?

Psalm. Look inside yourself. An eye has made
You deaf and blind: deaf to my cry
In things around you, blind to old texts prayed
By shapes of colours, things that lie,
By day, in pendent bells of words, and flit
As common pipistrelles, by night.
As thoughts gather I can delight
An ear planted so that I am of it.

II

Self. Those words of mine, they were not meant for you,
But this whole world, which isn't listening either.
What is it in my soul that listens to
This voice that I would give to you, that's neither
Yours nor mine, but planted in my ear?
What formed my eye that I shall see his word
Across the page one day like something I heard?
He that planted the ear shall he not hear?

And shall he need this work of mine one day?
Unless the Lord had been my help my soul
Had almost dwelt in silence. When I say
My foot slippeth I find his mercy holds
Me up. In the multitude of thoughts in this line
His comforts delight my soul. But who am I
To teach or chastise the world? I can but cry,
His gift lies buried in these words of mine.

95 ❧ Pastoral with a Horse-Chestnut Tree

While someone exhorts us
In song to sing to God,
I've looked askance and asked, is he
Among us here or not?
And found that question, off its no-man's land
Uptaken then in hand,

Lies with sheep in shade,
And takes its rest in space
Beneath a large-leafed chestnut, bright
With burning candles, placed
At intervals upon it, by that same hand,
Which forms from sea dry land.

Can it be we have
A second chance of rest?
I labour to hear a voice whose sworn
Obscurity you blessed,
Like a bright cloud above unharvested grain,
A clear heat after rain.

96 ❧ Bas-Relief

A voice inside my home
Had me rip our decking out, the end
Of this long winter, and dig a patch of ground
Inside its wooden frame:
I pulled bent nails like words the end of lines
And dug through nests to bricks I struck like rhymes
Scraping the edge of sound.

Later I opened your book
To read about the end of work, but caught
Instead the words, 'Thorns also and thistles', and thought
In passing of Eve's neck crooked,
Her slightly wry look, suckling, as Adam digs
Earth carved upon the haunch that's opposite,
Their writhing valley naught

But a grey spandrel, their sky
The slightly darker moulding of a sill
Above, rounded like bands of clouds on a hill
Moving invisibly.
Let this earth that's turned to words of love
In each new song herald such days as have
Already had their fill.

97 ❧ Nymphaeum

His house is this whole world, and its foundations,
Righteousness and judgment:
In my imagination,
A stuccoed seat upon a hill,
A temple fronted block his habitation,
Two dove cotes either side, the still
Apexes of wings outstretched and pendent.

Oh, yes, and dark clouds round that home:
Lightning lighting a nymphaeum,
A conduit and pool forever filled,
Hidden between the house and grove.
A proof becomes the owners of this pungent
Reality: the ghosts that move
From one end to the other,
Sowing light in love,
Happy these walls are fields, this earth their mother.

98 ❧ On the Flood Plain

Those things you fear, they have already happened,
Inside my contemplative soul,
Which left its bed, and came downstairs, to calm
Something I thought I must console:
The loud abandoned
Sounds of a woken Psalm.
But I was wrong: the cries of this song's voice
Are making a joyful noise.

Later a tall and white-haired neighbour knocked
Upon the door to that last stanza
To ask about my use of the word *soul*.
How could I know I'd have an answer
As I unlocked
The door to him, the whole
Structure quaking as I dared to put
On its threshold's wood his foot.

Let the roaring sea, which is this world,
Tumble, and all who sit inside
Its vast and half-transparent walls shall stand
And sing of that withdrawing tide:
The things it hurled
Behind it on the strand,

Archaic words that still deceive the eye
With their reality.

99 ❧ On a Solomonic Scale

I think of you against the sky among
Unrealized Portland cherubim,
Or stretched along
An unbuilt pediment to hear new hymns
Unsung behind the large square central space
Of this negative palace.

I think of you up there in space and know
That pillars of the Demiurge
(The portico
That was in fact once built to patch a church)
Were cracked by fire as stones flew like grenades
Above lead streams roofs made

And that the double cubes that make wondrous
Space behind a polychrome
Façade (that was
Later effaced) contain today no throne,
That façade once a king's final backdrop,
Hair tucked in his nightcap.

Even the stork up high has her agenda,
And swifts and swallows know the time,
After the end of
Winter, of their announcement of summer, but I'm
Certain, we only know the pitch of our
Judgment at the ninth hour:

It is a plan and elevation made
Before the building is begun,
Foundations laid
With each new life, the Temple of the Sun
And Moon each of us is, realized and baffled
At once upon the scaffold.

100 ⁊ Magnificat

I always try to stand as at the edge
Of dances, by the side of fizzing drinks,
　　　Against going in the first place,
And this work too is surly in its praise,
　　　　　A muttering thing that slinks
　　　　　　Away, or thinks
　　　It may do, waiting to be fetched.

I am, therefore, in need of exhortation
To sing, not murmur, this Magnificat.
　　　I am a mile beyond a long-
Gone gate, at which I see no sheep now throng.
　　　　　I am with outcasts sat
　　　　　　Whose dogs leap at
　　　No cheerful voice of your salvation.

Not me, but he who made us comfortless
No more, if each of us can leave behind
　　　This greedy, inconsolable,
Old world, and press a foot that leaps in the soul.
　　　　　I am the ways that wind,
　　　　　　The hidden sign:
'I am the way, the truth, and the life,' he says.

101 ⁊ Inside the Tympanum

　　　I went out once, came back at last,
　　　Only to find my radiant stanzas
　　　　　　Condensed to soiled
　　　　　Familiar phrases, souls
Of the earth's dust, oblivious of the hands as
Large as God's above that come to cast
　　　　　Us out, and pluck, and strum
　　　Upon this world, or tympanum.

I want to make this world a house
That can withstand us almost completely,
A place to know
By heart that in the glow
Of dusk quickens something into its mouse
Before lights are switched on, a thing that sweetly
Gnaws a cable, soon
Trapped, or drawn like leviathan.

102 ﷼ The Sparrow

A Penitential Psalm

Rebuilders of the book of John and Moses
Refused no stone, thank God,
To make a voice for us, in wildernesses
Of Antwerp, Rheims, Geneva,
In prison mumbling,
In fear and trembling,
The time it takes the weaver
To wake up in the wood,
The space of no career or priesthood.

Madly they hoped the ploughboy and the housewife,
The maid among the kine
And even the glowing traveller, the south side
Of the Downs, would hum
Unto the farms
New tunes for Psalms
As at the beam of the loom,
And souls would be refined
Threaded phrase by threaded line.

But did you let their cry come unto thee,
O Lord, and hear their prayer?

Incline an ear unto eternity
                    To ease a troubled heart:
                          Hide not thy face
                          These fragile days
                    That fall upon the hearth.
                    For I am lit with care
             That winds itself out everywhere.

And I have watched, and am become as a sparrow
                    Alone upon the lead.
O Lord, how amiable is this house, my narrow
                    Perch, thine holy book,
                          This sacred space
                          That owes its use
                    To nothing much: the nook
                    The swallow recoats for her bed,
The door through which thou shalt raise the dead.

103 ❧ Archaism

Those tiny figures of the middle ground;
The ones that take their burdened mules or asses
Across a bridge behind Ascanius' bow;
Or wash excess of dye from reddish cloth
Beneath a golden bridge in Lancashire,
As if they're princes bathing near Baghdad;
The one that toils almost invisibly
Beside two horses deftly conjured up
One summer afternoon in deepest Suffolk
Before the distant blue: if you step back
From peering at these forms quickly you'll see
Man's days are as a flower of the field
That flourishes, as grass wind passes o'er,
And then our places shall know us no more.
O earlier self that would advise its reader,

How can you make your poor lines end by saying:
'Man's days are as the grass wind passes o'er
And then our places shall know us no more'?
How can you make the least thing say these days,
To such as keep the word, it will endure,
From everlasting unto everlasting?

104 ❧ The Song of the Rising Sun

I

He who wishes to stay in the house of God
Must make his work like a band on tour up north:
        They take their stuff one sunny Sunday
              On a train down south, load
It on a porters' truck, and pull it forth,
Down empty aureate streets, to unload and play,
        In just one take, a song of, say,

He who covers himself with light, as with
A set of suits spotlit on stage, in halls
        And TV studios, who stretches
            Himself the curtains' width:
He who lets the beams of his chambers fall
Upon the waters, who walks the broken ledges
        Of hills and temples to catch in snatches

The song of the rising sun. And then they load
Their stuff again to play another gig
        Up north next day. When the truth is known
            The businessmen who owed
Them everything shall be cast out from this big
Enterprise of praising what is still stone
        Broke, for nothing you can own.

II

A thing of earth that breathes along this text
Is quickened in my consciousness as I
Murmur it out and wonder what comes next.
It's dawn, my blind is up, and I might spy
          A man that's wrapped in light
          As with a cloak
          To make eyesight
          A world on which to dart,
Chaos a spring on which wild asses look.

Birds sang and then it is the world's first night
After the day it took for the first harvest
To be created and then ripen: wheat
And vines and olives darken as all the forest
          Beasts creep forth from the wood
          And roaring lions
          Seek their food
          From God. 'The sun ariseth,'
And man is up to hunt leviathans.

105 ❧ Panel

This poem is the sequel to
          Some notes across the page
          I shall not show to you,
And to a vast historical
Song retelling miracles
          To this deaf age.

I've waited for this song and its son
          In indeterminate space
          Inside a lozenge on
A door, and watched it loitering
Beside a well, interpreting
          In prison, face

To face with Pharaoh once, or twice.
I've heard beside the shore
It sings its song inside
A song. But then I wandered off
And saw my notes, spaced, sleeping rough
Inside a door.

What have I to do with them?
These miracles and notes.
They wake and curse, and then
They stagger in their blanket up
To me and beg with crumpled cup,
Heads sore, and throats.

106 ❧ Companion

What can I do but make a dense
Precursor to a thing
That passed me on its way
Murmuring it had no change, and sing
The story of God's providence
Like yesterday.

You know I know the balancings
Of clouds and how our bones
Are made inside the womb,
But still you hurry from your homes.
I lie and drink and beg from things
Above in whom

I have my being: all you that say
You have no change, or cast
Your bread upon the face
Of my chaos, and like that last
Poem are bent on getting away
Back to your place.

This poem has a lost companion
　　　　Panel, which tells, I'm told,
　　　　The story of the people's
Rebellion, and in that old
Story the earth's a sudden canyon,
　　　　　　A rift that ripples.

BOOK FIVE

107 ❧ *Before the Sons of Men*

I

Give thanks unto the self-consuming god
That's lying by the road, who manifests
Himself eternally, almost on the nod,
　　　　This pavement's edge his wilderness.
Put back that smashed gorilla glass you tip
To your bent face, and stop awhile, he'll strip
The copper from your dome and marvel at
The orders on your life as if you are
Their perfect microcosm and he was sat
　　　　Upon the bronze of a toppled car.
O that men *praised this God in wondrous works*
　　　　Before the sons of men.

This flesh, my family, your commonplace
Opinion, the very need I seem
To have for money, O, the time it takes
　　　　For me to earn it. Such a dream
I've had as hardens to Carrara stone
Unfinished in a studio: the bone
My flesh still veils beneath its rasping wave.
These things are hard enough material
To be my words, which take the form of a slave
　　　　Being born at burial.
O that men *praised this God in wondrous works*
　　　　Before the sons of men.

113

They that take a flight, for business or pleasure,
From Tokyo and from Los Angeles,
From Reykjavik and Santiago, they measure
       God's works, his wonders on the seas,
In air miles. Weight of air rushes to fill
The space through which they speed and drinks are spilled.
They mount up to the heaven: they go down to
The depths again. A hostess staggers like
A drunken man, a woman in the loo
       Is at her wit's end, 'for God's sake.'
O that men *praised this God in wondrous works*
       Before the sons of men.

II

He turns a land of aqueducts and fountains
       And irrigated terraces
Into a land of ruined templates, rocks,
       And rusticating surfaces,
A land where sun-kissed soffits give themselves
       In time to winds and sand and things
That bask and hiss upon them, undisturbed
       By men who used to dwell therein.
Like rhymes eroded by a later time,
       Its new style of pronunciation
Or loss of letters maybe, blocks upon
       This space in my imagination
Are pastoralized into massy repoussoirs
       Before a newly luscious plain.
Winds stir. A figure comes and draws a bow
       As prototype of Charlemagne
And suddenly his empire mushrooms to
       New York, Milan and Singapore.
Whoso is wise and will observe those things
       Discerns our likeness to the Lord.

108 ❧ Loot
Of David

Just like this Psalm my mind's made up
Of parts of other texts:
Just like this Psalm I am determined,
'O God, my heart is fixed'.
Book three was finished yesterday, book two
Two days before, and now

I find I have one hundred Psalms
In all, I thought to myself,
Crawling on quasi-rhymes, to steal
The harp from off the shelf:
Picked up from off the table, struck with fear,
Its words are in my ear.

I struggled with their hope, these lines,
Then raced to work, my route
Across a park towards a cedar,
My mind burdened with loot
As I walked, when to my eye an eagle cropped
That cedar, took its top-

Most branch, its tender twigs, into
An arid land of start-
Up businesses, a four-square city
With money at its heart:
Majestic companies busy like Mammon
Exiling its river's salmon.

'Vain is the help of man': I'll take
That line and plant it firm
In lofty soil of this one hundred-
Year-old lyric form,
The invention of a man, forlorn at fifty,
Counting what leaves us swiftly.

Two-for-One
Of David

          Short lines came first:
A cento of retributive rhetoric
I put in the shape of a cross, like someone burst
          Asunder, picked
          From out the mud
          Of fields of blood:
          It's going to
          Take a while.
      We've got a job to do.
      We will not rest. And I'll
          Stand by your grave.
          I'll do such things.
          The old men rave.
          The young man sings.
I thought, *this scripture must have been fulfilled,*
And wrote, *the holy Ghost and Word that killed,*
To gird myself and mount the horse of my
Attempt to curse and find an enemy:
          The mouth of Satan
          Is open for business,
          His global nation
          Screwing listless
          Punters sideways
          Everywhere.
I wrote. Then copied out, *O God of my praise,*
To try and work out how he *hears my prayer,*
The subject of my curse becoming clearer,
Quite literally, as Satan's mouth came nearer:
          His tongue untied
          Splits signifier
          From signified,
          And high-paid liars
          Perpetuate
          His crime in discourse
          That would negate
          All order for us.

O how lost, I thought, *archaic notions*
Are across our dark and *rising oceans*,
And then, with half an eye upon the Psalm,
I let the cursing start, quite unalarmed:

> *Let such a liar*
> *Be judged, condemned,*
> *Dragged to the pyre*
> *To make his end.*
> *Let Satan stand*
> *Inside the flames*
> *At his right hand*
> *And let his name*
> *Be blotted out.*

I said. *Let strangers spoil his labour and rout*
His work. A battle's aftermath in mind,
Its soil and blood, because I had a rhyme.
Right then I understood the purpose of
This cursing, whom it was I cursed, the love
Involved in my short lines: it was my own
Soul's faculties I fought, my will that groans
Face down in mud, my memory and its
Bedraggled forms, their implements in bits,
That I must put to rout, and reason in
A room inland, pretending to be king,
But fearing seers, the thing to be usurped,
The sceptre put from him and powers curbed.
When I have made such inroads that I see
And feel my heart is wounded within me,
Then I am gone, a shadow that declines,
As black as curses with or without rhymes.
Let these diversifying faculties
Be clothed with shame: let my adversaries
Run from my words haphazardly through earth
So I may witness finally the birth
Of something unexpected in these lines,
Which fills their dark intent with light and shines
With such exuberance I am become

A kind of nothingness inside the hum
Of words the other side of words that curse:
A king troubled before the fabled birth.

110 ❧ Hapax Legomenon

Of David

They say the thing no longer is of use
            When it's inside those walls
            That echo with footfalls
Of visitors. Likewise, this old, obtuse,
Corrupted text: its critical edition
            Footnotes it to perdition.

Or not quite yet. Out of what might just be
            An old scribe's carelessness,
            The dittographic mess
Of a hapax legomenon, I see
A royal figure come: like night the day tricks,
            This ancient text's its matrix.

As words are from the heart so offspring are,
            Laboriously, from
            The womb. The temple's gone
In which this Psalm was first performed. Not far
Above our feet, in inhospitable space,
            The words remake their place.

111 ❧ The Stone-Fly

Since you secured my freedom and led me out
Into the midst of waters upon dry ground
Away from several generations bound
Progressively by cosmopolitan doubt

And free emotive verse; since you have made
The olive leaves of your book so many quails
For me to tear and eat when my strength fails
And I'm murmuring at you; and since you've laid
Your letters on my heart, effaced them too,
Promised me a land I might discern:
I'll cast this line again and hope you'll turn
And strike the dry mayfly I made for you.
Fear of the Lord is rock that's struck in two,
And on its shoals, I look and reel and learn.

112 ❧ Later Commentary

He lost it all and then was given twice
As much as he had before. (I'll take that stack
Of cash. Hm. That gold earring. Very nice.
And thank you much.) But who would give it back—
Six thousand camels, all those flocks and herds—
For one last hand of everlasting verse.

He has dispersed, he's given to the poor,
They'll say, and then they'll ask to see the hand
Of verse that he had in return. The law
Of words in rhyme is not a game we planned,
They'll say, to play all night, on which we'll stake
All that we have. Come on. Give us a break.

Explain these images. What kind of game
Is it you're playing with us? (I didn't think
It even was a game at first.) The same
Deal with the one before. How could we drink
From out its rock? And what odd fish, dear fisher,
Did you expect to reel from out its minute fissure?

The wicked shall see it and be grieved, he'll gnash his teeth
And melt away, just like these images

Into each other, nuances beneath
Their riches, hidden meanings dropped to fizz
Inside your glass, like wild excuses made
By later commentary for what's being said.

113 ⁓ Magnificat

I'll shake onto this page the dried foodstuff,
The fluff and tiny objects something swept
Up overnight into the corners of
My mind, the bits and pieces that were kept
Then lost, making these lines, as reason leapt
In its womb: I'll take this precious stuff and grind
It to a kind of dust that speaks its mind,

And try and make amends in these poor lines
For the Magnificat I didn't say
At my son's baptism, knowing nothing shines
Like commendation in the mouths of grey
Impossible mothers, who've set each day
Above the price of tomorrow, and kept death
Rapt at the door, still listening for our breath.

114 ⁓ The Order of the Psalms

The singing of the Psalm was like a hand
That took a book and chanced upon the place
It sought at once. They sang as if I'd planned
To make these lines today. And in that space
Of Purbeck shafts, that land inside a land
That several choirs had filled, you hid your face.
Why should I spell it out. How strange the text
They sang last night should be, as I'd planned, mine next.

I stood inside that space as if I was
Between two lines and heard 'The Table for
The Order of the Psalms' dispel that pause,
At watch, discretely prompting at its door,
That pause a terrifying wilderness
That is just sensed upon stage or sea floor.
Between the lingua franca of our age
And your kind words I circle across this page.

115 ❧ *Montagne Sainte-Victoire*

The Bible is
A thing like nature
A man gets up day after
Day to paint, hounded by boys
The end of his days on his way to paint the breadth
Of the same old outcrop, its rugged height and depth.

An obstinate man
Who has progressed
Very slowly, blessed
With jagged nature realized on
Rectangles, he sees sensations of colour give light,
Someone's black stroke a failure he must at all costs fight.

Another man,
Just as obstinate,
Will say to you how obvious
It is that colours depend on
Form or outline and how the quarrel between
The Florentine and Titian determines the vision seen.

The Bible is
The look of heaven
On earth that has been given

To children of men, a thing of bliss
That takes our finitude while we have it
And colours it into something that's infinite.

116 ꠲ The Oracles of God

Old songs were on his mind as he wrote his letter,
Like an unrealized idea
An artist melts inside the motif's weather,
And sounded in his ear,
Like lines joined up
Across a gap
In space or time, to make the subject matter.

The Oracles of God are on a plain
Of colours on a canvas.
He has renounced the hidden things of shame,
Not painting a stone acanthus.
And I should make,
For your dear sake,
Another discontinuous line to explain.

The whole of nature's in the scoop of a cup,
A substance being handed
Out to flocking guests by a man made up
Of yesterday, a man dead,
Or so I thought
When I had fought
My way to him across the smoky hubbub.

I started suddenly from what had seemed
To last a hundred years,
A vast and faceted and tan-hued dream,
And said all men are liars:
I love because
What comes to pass
Shall take my voice, this sawn-up seasoned beam.

117 ❧ Extravagant Doxology

Under my neighbour's vine,
And under his fig tree,
I beat into a pruning hook or line
Extravagant doxology
To cut branches that have emerged
Over my fence,
Spewing sense
From sides of a mouth, as if I am being purged:
Since you were kind enough to take
With us your rest,
Let apprehension wake
To try and sound its guest.

118 ❧ The Stone Set at Naught

I
TEST

News of you is like
A half-planned boat ride
Around a nearby island,
The cliffs the sea's side

To our surprise are crowned
With tropical
Cacti, plump, untroubled
And edible

But hostile to the touch,
The climate heady
And foreign to us although
We're abroad already.

You are the stone that is set
At naught, the one

That shall crown the quoins, and the sun
        Behind the sun

That rises to its vanishing
        Each august at dawn;
A dream I had of something
        That struggled to its form

From out a foot of mine
        In utter agony,
Three magpies looking on
        With eyes of money.

II
SCAN

In white or grey, beneath
        The rough voussoirs,
By undressed stone, in dresses
        Azure or turquoise,

Stand mostly familiar figures,
        Five, once to me,
The most familiar,
        Now less three.

Although I knew the wall
        Was very old,
I did not ever go there,
        And used to hold

The figures photographed
        Against it,
More permanent, somehow bound
        To outlast it.

Sound of the waves before
        And after our
Short holiday, for untold
        Millennia,

Sight of the womb's night sky
    Without its creature,
Teach me about another
    Kind of future

When we are gone before
    The keystone or quoin
All the stones the builders
    Turned down.

119 ❧ *Aleph, Beth, Gimel, Daleth*

I found a precept in a rhyme, and laws
Of yours inside a name on a boat's prow
As I passed by, a word that made me pause,
Which someone said without them knowing how
They spoke to me, but finally no cause,
Just proof that all creation, then and now,
Is made of meaningful coincidence,
Reality, of strange significance.

Wherewithall shall I be clothed? With what translucence?
By concentrating hard on making art
'According to thy word', I sought a new sense
Of words or things unseen with my whole heart,
And I rejoiced that money's just a nuisance,
No medium I need to make a start:
Its lack, translucently, a living thing
That acts upon my mind to make me sing.

Behold the fowls of the air and how they fly
Or sing apart from us. The words I put
Together are a kind of path that I
Might stray as far and catch a stranger's foot
That climbs up there on gold behind the sky,
A child on a blue thigh, me clutching loot.

That stranger stands at my door and strings a shell.
My words would hear what he has made of hell.

You spat and made me cleave unto the dust
Of literal significance. I see
That ground quicken and wonder if I must
Now try and justify the fantasy
Of that last verse whose gold begins to rust
To bole below, like rubbed reality.
These lines abide your synchronicities
Like nameless acts a spaced-out beggar sees.

He, Vav, Zain

Shoulder my words back into a range whence
I've strayed, these stacks of lines of mine a hod
Of images of lost significance.
Loose from the string stretched on the bow you trod
And bent a new-fletched shaft of sudden sense:
Your target shifts upon this verse, my God.
Revive these tercets rooted in your word
Like some old tale I must have once misheard:

'*Even* thy salvation according to thy word.'
Let your mercies come and all those other
Archaic-sounding things I've read or heard,
And I shall walk at large one way or another,
To seek a rhyme or precept, undeterred
By rhymes or precepts, all the pain and bother
Of putting verse together without bright things
On earth of which a tuneful person sings.

And who would then deride the way I cling
To your and others' words as if I were
Attempting here an unattempted thing
In rhyme or quasi-rhyme, my words from her
Who played about your feet, of whom they sing
Or used to sing so madly everywhere.
These words boil over from some words I left,
And then forgot, like precepts made bereft.

Cheth

It wasn't at midnight, but two a.m.,
When I awoke to write this verse, a spell
That's tied me back to back with them
That live inside your limbs, these rhymes a hell
From which I would escape by the dawn I am
Become that lights the night into which I fell,
And now I see fingers have come to scrawl
Upon the frescoes on this crumbling wall.

Teth, Iod

I thought I'd write a version of the longest
Of all the Psalms in stanzas of ottava rima.
Blithely I let my lines unfold along its
Old acrostic precepts like a dreamer
Who dreams the book on his lap is the strongest
Hypnotic known to man, so strong it seemed a
Richer thing than gold or silver's strange
Reality, the world I'd hoped to change.

But who in that greasy reality
Would want to read such stanzas in any case?
'Let the proud be ashamed' she cannot see
They'd work outside their context: I'll meditate
'In thy precepts'. Your hands have fashioned me,
'And the Word was made flesh', and dwelt among us to grace
Our words with truth: stanza by stanza they
Remake a place I'll let so it'll not decay.

Caph, Lamed, Mem

Me. Me. Me. Quicken me. A voice like wine
Inside my skin matures into the fruit
That is its origin. It is a vine-
Cutter's song that played about a foot
Half-lifting on a vat, a prophet's line
Like shouting for the summer fruit being cut

And singing that ceased that might yet call the earth
Vivaciously from age back to its birth.

Man is a poem that's mostly in your head,
Some parts already noted down, no rhymes
In place as yet, his theme the end of a thread
You wind around a form's old precepts, lines
And lines of him, their way of being said
A sphere eventually of earth that shines:
Or so you hope; my lines I see are quickened
By roots of precepts drunk on loam that thickens.

My teachers would have had me learn about
The room, in which we sat, to try and figure
Out, once I'd measured it, its price, no doubt
To sell it and buy another, similar, bigger.
But I would leave the friends and books I bought
Along the way, my very home, to kick a
Gate open on the distances I've heard
It said are massed like honey in your word.

Nun

I woke at four, in June, to go downstairs
And write this verse, my mind conflicted, my soul
Glistening and twisted upon the bed I share
Inside the curve of my protruding sole.
The other side, in pollinating air,
A river god writhed round from gold on bole.
At last I stumbled down to find my text:
'Thy word's a lamp to my feet, a light to my steps.'

Samech

I hate the lazy atheist and writer
Of childish anecdotal verse, the half-
Hearted distracted souls I find inside a
Magazine or class these days, who laugh
Their way inside my head at last, the better

To fill the space I lack with dross and fluff:
'I am the true vine and my father is
The husbandman,' he says, and the world hates this.

Ain, Pe

At dawn I seek for hours a kingdom on
My couch, before they wake and ask what we
Shall eat right now, my wife and little son,
His smaller brother too, whose 'me, me, me'
And greedy hands reach up to things upon
My heart like yours making reality.
Money made the world they snatched last night:
I brush the crumbs from off my couch and write.

I haven't rioted for years, drunk wine
For months, but I cry out and stagger slightly.
The spirit of deep sleep, a bore of brine,
Covers my rapid eyes so very lightly,
And I can see your book in my eyes' mind,
Letters that cannot be deciphered quietly:
The swelling estuary of your words spreads light
On my grey mud and sand the more of it I write.

Tsaddi

Like God, I'm jealous: my love for you's intense.
I cannot bear to see you live without
Chapter and verse. I hate your ignorance
Of our high and holy book, your clever doubt
Of which I am compounded too, against
My better judgment, base angel and lout
Embracing in this furnace, to which I add
Reducing substances, my words so much slag.

Koph, Resh, Schin, Tav

Morning after morning I find that I'm
Awake before the dawn quietly to cry

'I hoped in thy word'. Through matins, lauds, and prime,
I sit upon my couch, mumbling, that I
'Might meditate in thy word', and make my time
A kind of endless compline, my thoughts held high
Enough, I hope, for seraphim to hear,
And tricksters too, spewing leaves, as you draw near.

I hammer out your lines like someone stood
At an old piano mimicking a star,
Who dressed and sang and lived as if he could
Take on the dust's sincerity, in a bar,
Out on the road, beyond a native wood:
Clothes and voice and face transfigured far
Inside the lights, tunes hammered out I've heard
That quicken me according to your word.

Your word is on my mind, a worm that's hearsed
Inside a blackbird's beak, not dead but coiled
Proleptically as I begin this verse
And rejoice through prime as one that finds great spoil.
Your word is pulled at dawn and thrust head first
Into a mouth that's stretched from vault to soil.
I cannot see which end's the head, the tail,
If it's a worm or coin or old wives' tale.

Let my cry come near: give me your word.
I've heard it said my lips and tongue were changed,
As in a tale, from prisoners to bird:
Let me live in these less obvious chains
Of talon, beak and feather, reassured
This image is but sky through which I've ranged.
I've gone astray like a strange shifting thing:
Seek out what cries from rhymes I'd be following.

120 ❧ Transfiguration

A Song of Ascents

If I have cried in my distress
It would have been a flippant 'O God!'
Or 'Christ!' A cry of helplessness
You didn't hear. But then I witnessed

Three men spotlit on stage, a cloud
That shadowed us, a voice, they say,
From out that cloud, which overawed
My understanding, the ground we trod

In our shoes holy ground. You lay
A reddened coal of juniper
Upon my tongue. I must obey.
'Here am I.' I cry. The tray

Of breakfast things I'm righting for her
Turned from. Mouth dry. I see I'm dressed
As in a novel. A cat might purr
Around my feet. I hear her 'Gurrhr!'

121 ❧ Eyes Unseen

A Song of Ascents

A hoof troubles the edge,
A cloud drifts in its sheen:
The book lies open on my lap
And lifts its eyes unseen
To look up where my lost intentions range,
The hills in which they're changed.

Great works like that, inside
My head's deep space, I've chained,
And will not suffer a foot to be moved,

Nor rhyme to be exchanged
For them. Beneath a stone they run out clean
Or clear as sources I've seen.

122 ✤ Old Red Sandstone

A Song of Ascents

I'd say her light was like conglomerate stone
That's quarried locally
To make grey-green and red and purplish brown

Imposts and tracery,
Now ruined or lost or lying in someone's house
Unceremoniously

As a chimney's lintel and jambs. Her mouth's
A mandorla that lacks
Its Christ as she lies by my side, whose whereabouts

She's dreaming of. Poor shacks
And shrubs grew up, and then were cleared, from her limbs
Or walls. In chimneystacks

Her dress has been transfigured. Two roes that are twins
Shall feed in her nave or lawn
Sometimes at dawn in the place of chants and hymns.

123 ✤ 'As lively pupils'

A Song of Ascents

As lively pupils lift their tender eyes
Into the eyes of their first teacher once
She's cried at them to hush their cries;
As grey-haired people go to halls in herds,

In pairs, or alone, to make an audience,
And gaze upon a man some idolize:

So my eyes wait for signs and glints
Of you in all these cloudy skies of words.

We are those words: 'have mercy upon us.'
Our soul is scorned by those that are at ease,
        And that contempt sends us from whence
We were sent, poor in spirit, but yours, 'O Lord.'

124 ࿓ The Brave Little Tailor
A Song of Ascents

        If it had not been that I sought first
The kingdom of God, as in a fairy tale
        A man or boy or tailor sets off
                And cannot fail
To win the hand to half, the wedding chest
        Of its reluctant and radiant princess:

        If it had not been that I sought first
Thing this morning, I say, the kingdom of God,
        Then the waters had overwhelmed us,
                And I'd have trod
The eyes that blink inside my pan in pain,
        And grabbed a rope of pearls in vain.

        Then I'd have drunk a bitter cup
This morning, quickly caught up, back and forth,
        In a raging torrent you walked upon,
                About the fourth
Watch of the night, and you'd have passed us by
        Had you not heard my troubled cry.

        Our soul is escaped as a bird escapes
Taxonomy inside a lucent dream.
        With hardly any feathers left
                That it can preen,
It sees itself in what it sought at last:
        A jewel that asks what it has asked.

125 ❧ Their Old *Rifugio*
A Song of Ascents

They that seek your kingdom first
Must have an antiquated look
In the eyes of this long-cultivated world
On its wide plain. Up there before the peak—

Surrounded as it is by mountains of you,
    The cairns and treks you'd have us make
To get there and build it or spend the night—
    Their old *rifugio* must take

In their imagination quite a battering,
As in reality it makes storms speak,
    And gives to snow that stays the summer
    The look of vellum scraped for a book.

126 ❧ 'I read a Psalm and I am like'
A Song of Ascents

I read a Psalm and I am like
    Them that dream;
They live a proverb not a life.
    With tears in my eyes
I come across a famous line
    And straightaway
Its bright proliferations light
    My dreaming mind.
It is the flower looked for that lies
    Scattered on
A scree. Wrathful like a lion
    In a tourist's proverbs.
Or in a loving letter alive
    With attitudes

Of mind that lounge like skin in lime.
        The excess of it
Like erratics on wide arable land
        Or a poetics
Whose lines are littered with the word *like*.

127 ❧ At the Limits of the Eye
A Song of Ascents

This is the line, the block that was
        Inside the grass, upbuilt
Before it fell, was stumbled on,
        Which I might raise or tilt
To see what doesn't love it: some might guess
        The lord that built the house.

It's vain for you to rise up early
        From table, bed or hill,
To sit in semi-listlessness
        And mumble lines until
They're merely sounds inside a mouth of sorrows,
        Which look so strange tomorrow:

Unless a stranger walk the city,
        The watchmen watched in vain.
Unless I rearticulate
        That hard, old-fashioned name
For that which lives at the limits of the eye,
        How can he hear the cry?

The Lord provides for those he loves,
        The seed planted in sleep.
Children are the fruit of a womb
        As sounds of scattered sheep
Are formed from a textile pattern, the bright horizon
        On the shoulders of a season.

128 * *Inclusio*
A Song of Ascents

Prosperous that man whose fear of the Lord
Makes him alliterative and almost rhyme,
Whose opening word shall be a Psalm's first word,
Whose wife is like a fruitful vine

That peeps and crawls into his window,
Whose children are like shoots of olive trees
Around his table, on his knees,
Inside that happy song's *inclusio*.

Prosperous that man whose fear of the Lord
Becomes, like all of us in long lost time,
The medium in which he lives, the word
That gives our world its final rhyme.

129 * The Light of the World
A Song of Ascents

I've read it out for years, that line about
The grass upon the housetops,
Which withers before it grows up,
'Whereof the mower filleth not
His hand, nor he that takes its sheaves his bosom.'

I've read it out to groups and it has blossomed
Inside that 'palpable
Interpretation' I'll
Have grabbed from the sill, the criticism
As quaint as the painting it would have us love:

'The Light of the World', inside its chapel of
A chapel, by a door,—
Or portal to a shore

Of herbs spontaneously above
The taste of them and salt and lemon trees

The colour of faded tufts a poet sees
Giving to bricks and curbstones
The look of sundrenched home,
As if sunlight lived there, like seas,
Which dream for miles of taking hold of heaven.

130 ❧ A Penitential Psalm
A Song of Ascents

Working my way
Through the Songs of Ascents,
My head and heart already on holiday,
Upon a path that runs through terraces,
Spilling themselves, like shelves of scent
Of herbs and citruses
A hand has swept across and smashed,
I found I reached the penitential calm
Of Lent's penultimate Psalm,
My version of it against a wall, trashed.

Trashed and crying
Out of the depths
It must have taken most of the night trying
To reach, alone, out in the bars about
The town, I guess, its vows unkept
Because Lent's gone, no doubt.
I'll wait with it the rest of the night.
It is a voice, which lacks salt, that I must stir,
To which I add salt, a year
And a day, tasting to get it just right, or upright.

Out of the depths I cried to you:
Hear my voice and lend an ear.

137

If you should watch and mark iniquity
    Who stands? Forgive and then you're feared.

I wait and wait and hope for word,
    'More than they that watch for the morning':
Let us hope in loving kindness, '*I say*,
    More than they that watch for the morning'.

131   A Simile
A Song of Ascents

The hour it turned my wife's saint's day,
    The latent phase began,
        And like a man
Superfluous, I was happily labouring away
    At the final lines of a Song of Ascents
        I'd happened upon by chance.

'Children are the fruit of a womb,'
    I'd mused, words milling about,
        As I figured out—
Unlike my wife who was draped as on a tomb—
    That image macrocosmically
        Inside a simile.

A simile that greets me as
    An unruly mini-me
        These days, quite free
Of my exacting comprehension, alas:
    A child that is weaned of his mother
        And simply adores his brother.

Broken slightly by his moods
    I am no longer haughty
        As he is naughty
In a charming manner, crying now for food.

As he's grown up, Psalm after Psalm,
He's made my heart quite calm.

132 ? Ephrata
A Song of Ascents

We heard of it at Ephrata,
The place you put down as your place of birth,
Whose root is fruitfulness. We found it in
The fields of the wood, and now we know that earth
Is filled with this impossibility
As the waters cover the sea.

I'll not stay under my covers
The early hours: I will not sleep or rest
Until I know what it is I'm looking for.
I've heard it said the wind at dawn confessed
To listening leaves knowledge of God. But I
Shan't judge with ear and eye.

I see and hear instead
A sun that rises as a sucking child
That plays on the hole of the asp, and puts his hand,
When he is weaned, upon the den of the mild
And venomous adder: a branch that writhes
Out of the womb of night.

133 ? 'Deep calleth unto Deep'
A Song of Ascents

I stand inside your simile inside
A simile
And see 'Deep calleth unto deep', one foot
On shore and one in mist like sea.

As one secluded mountain's mist descends
                    Upon another
Like oil that drips on a dusty hem from hair
          And beard of a priest and ancient brother:

Behold, brothers, how pleasant and good it is
                    To dwell together
In unity that's fast anointing us
          Like holy and indifferent weather.

134 ☙ Finisterre

A Song of Ascents

                    I've watched, and cringed to see,
Exuberant actors raise their hands and shout,
          Expressing glee or joy or something,
          And I have tried to iron out
          The creases of emotion from
All crumpled recitations of a poem.

                    In Santiago I found a room,
And then got up to walk to Finisterre,
          And when I'd reached the stone lighthouse
          And pounding waves that I found there,
          I took a bus and plane back home,
Rereading still the battered epic poem

                    That I had carried there.
I step on heaven's azure in trepidation
          And steal archaic lapis, carefully
          Hiding the wondrous sense of elation
          I feel as I at night alone
Complete creation in Zion, or this scrunched poem.

135 ⁊ Chryselephantine

                    This song outlingers
                    What it decries.
Its non-invisible material
Makes time, which murmurs close, fall through the eyes
                    And mind of all
                    Its freshest singers
                    Until their mouth
Has filled the pool of an ear in its deep drouth.

            This song decries work of men's hands:
            Chryselephantine heathen idols,
            Now broken up, bartered, and lost,
            Or catalogued and lying idle
            In each city's museum I
            Must really visit one of these days.

            The time it takes to murmur this song
            Is time enough for breath that plays
            Upon original chaos
            To play upon the chaos each
            Of us shall bring to it, to make
            A languid river god half-reach
            For air and fall and rise again.
            Our language is the medium
            Of God in time, not gold and ivory,
            Nor glass and aluminium.

136 ⁊ 'I' ho già fatto un gozzo in questo stento'

The time it takes to murmur out this Psalm
Is time enough to ask, what man is this
Rebuking time until there is a calm.

Like one of Ocean's sons drunk on his farm,
I stir from self-induced paralysis,
The time it takes to murmur out this Psalm,

And curse the Fall of Man, the ancient harm
To which I came last night, a morning kiss
Rebuking time until there is a calm.

It is a languid river god, embalmed
In sweat, who's laid upon the grassy abyss,
The time it takes to murmur out this Psalm,

Who stirs and stretches arms as if he'd charm
The sun from out the moon, his yawning gnosis
Rebuking time until there is a calm.

Breath of my mouth obeys the stretched-out arm
Of words in time and I pass through the midst,
The time it takes to murmur out this Psalm,
Rebuking time until there is a calm.

137 ❧ Pseudepigrapha

I

If I begin this song where it must end,
                    O daughter of Babylon,
You may not a hear a famous tune or two,
Although I promise you, you'll know this one,
                    But happy shall he be
                    That recompenses you.
                    You made my land a strange land
                    And took it from me:
            I'll take the songs you thought you knew
                    And make them strange to you.
A prophet springs and curses from out the ashes
            Of Burns and The Melodians:

'Happy shall he be
That taketh and dasheth
Thy little ones against the stones.'

How shall we sing the Lord's song in a strange land?
Your land—my land—this land
To which I'm brought by industry and science,
Which has progressed from excellence
To empty excellence.
This land shall be to you
As when God overthrew
Sodom and Gomorrah.
Dragons shall cry in towers of offices
And satyrs shall dance there.
It shall be more horrible
Than avant-garde collages,
Than the dark fantastic mess
Of a modern science fiction novel
Or trilogy of purgatorial dreams
In which what is becomes what seems.

A girl with teeth of frozen
Saliva curses and ahoys,
On a ship at sea, a busy boatswain,
And then there is a tempestuous noise.

Let the words of our mouth
And the meditation of our heart
Be acceptable in thy sight
Here tonight.

By the rivers of Babylon
Where we sat down
There we wept
When we remembered Zion.

It must be Moses made the Pentateuch,
　　　　And most, or all, the Book of Psalms
　　　　　Is made from David's poems or songs:
And do not be surprised to learn it took
　　　　Just a day, the same eighth day,
　　　　To make these books of fire and clay.

Like Jacob on his beanstalk, which Jack felled,
　　　　Behold, they put some stones for pillows,
　　　　They took their harp from off the willows,
And climbed all day to take the giant's gold:
　　　　They sang above the sea and longed
　　　　To have the Lord their strength and song.

138 ❧ The Song of the Frog
Of David

　　　　　　The future is immense,
　　　Some time ago, a poet said,
　　　　　　And David prophesied once,
　　　'All kings of the earth shall praise thee, God.'
Where are these kings today? Art thou in space?
　　　Who or what has taken thy face?

　　　　　　I thought that there must be
　　　Some kind of answer in the tale
　　　　　　Of David silenced by
　　　The frog a Sea-beast swallows whole,
Whose song surpasses his. I write it out
　　　And have, like God in man, no doubt.

　　　　　　'I will praise thee with my
　　　Whole heart', with lines that burst through cracks
　　　　　　Along my days. I cry
　　　As pungently by night. Like Jack-
By-the-hedge or ancient herbs in railway cuttings
　　　Thy lines decultivate in my muttering.

139 ❧ In San Luigi dei Francesi

Of David

The hand that moves toward the lines to come
　　To wake them from their hidden state
　　　　Of somnolent ekphrasis—
　　　　　　This hand that passes
　　　　　　Beyond its weight—
　　Is not God's, I notice, but the one
　　　　Adam reclined upon
When he'd proffered himself for God to create.

This heavy object raised by Christ to call
　　Matthew in the sudden sunlight
　　　　Is David's too, a size
　　　　　　Beyond his thighs:
　　　　　　It is the straight right,
　　The hand that makes you capable,
　　　　Like children of light in Paul,
Of proving what's acceptable in God's sight.

The conflict in the chiaroscuro's fierce,
　　And never stops, and is between
　　　　Man and God: the Prince
　　　　　　Of the Air that thinks
　　　　　　He's made of man
　　A house that's safe from fears,
　　　　A place to spend his nights and purse,
And light that strikes such wealth or mirth within.

Say I took the wings of dawn to follow
　　The line of waves way out at sea;
　　　　Went up to heaven and said
　　　　　　I'll make my bed
　　　　　　In Hell to see
　　What I can dream down there or swallow:
　　　　Even then, I find my pillow
Shines as the day, and thy right hand shall hold me.

140 ⅋ One Click
Of David

One click and I had bought a groaning sorrow
     With free one-day delivery.
               Pick me tomorrow
          In thy fulfilment centre:
            Deliver me
      Through streets and fields of winter,
             Is what it sings.

I'm overthrown. My goings are in hands
     Of strangers. Carelessly I'm tossed in
             The backs of vans
        Where I'm in danger of
           Going missing,
       Handled without love,
           Among cold things.

It snowed meanwhile and still I wait to take
     Delivery of this pure song.
            Let coals be raked
       To burn up what it is
          That takes so long
      To come and speak its bliss,
          The life it brings.

141 ⅋ Delicacies of this Fat Age
Of David

          Judges in hands of crags . . .
May smite me . . . the righteous . . . loving kindness . . . an axe
          Has struck this text:
          Its things lie scattered
As shards of words of bone about the cleft
        Of its hard subject matter.

My text's corrupted too
As I make it almost appeal to you.
Let me not eat
Delicacies
Of this fat age, or make my hard work sweet,
Unlike these prophecies.

Tending my plump words
Upon a nearby slope, I watched my herd
Fall suddenly
Inside this cleft.
Or was it that they ran into the sea,
Like legions made bereft

And overthrown on earth,
To rise, like angels witnessing your birth.
What shall I sing
To them, these angels,
But words on my tongue, the strokes that swell to wings,
Then slip to puffed triangles.

142 ❧ *De Antro Nympharum*
Of David

I

Walking northwards through city streets at noon,
The sky a capping
Of crease limestone,
I did not watch my breath, and cares came lapping
Against the inside bends of my mind's course,
And lay in point bar thoughts.

I looked on my right hand and saw a tree
Pregnant with buds
Suddenly
Lit up against a park's stained crags of clouds.
I thought I'll plant this tree where there was none,
In ground above this song.

II

I cried with my own voice:
With my own voice I made
This book of supplications I'm
Certain is almost finished,
And into which you vanished,
Like someone with no choice,
Like some old shade,
Or words that merely rhyme.

I cried, 'I cried unto thee',
Trouble and persecution
Wait for you in the cave of this heart.
But what went in in fear
And trembling reappeared
Transfigured as at the
Initiation
Of some invisible art.

'Deliver me', I've risen
To say, for I am brought
Very low inside this book,
Or supplicating poem,
'That I may praise thy name',
Bring my soul out of prison:
My spirit was caught
To be held up by your hook.

143 ❧ A Penitential Psalm

Of David

Do you have faith in me? Then hear my prayer.
Or did you take the shape of every child
That's born, and grow up through two thousand years,
Only to hatch a plot to have me killed?
My eyes are overwhelmed: I see no God.

My ears are desolate: I hear of none.
But then the blackbird sings his infinite song:
I see the blossoms snow on paths you trod.
I remember the days of old and meditate
On all your works, the work of your skilled hands,
And stretch forth my blind hands to pray and take:
My soul thirsts after you as a thirsty land.

Hear quickly the headlong fall of my poor words,
Hide not your face from them lest they assume
The haggard face of office-going herds
That hurry on down as if to be exhumed.
Cause me to hear your loving kindness this morning:
I trust that I will lift myself in such talk.
Pull me from plots of those without your learning:
Cause me to know the way to take my walk.
Teach me to act with your imagination.
Lead me into the land of prophecy.
Quicken me with honest indignation.
I am that man that I might write and see.

144 ❧ The Prophet Daniel
Of David

In the third year of writing from thy book,
        I'll make again a new
            Song unto thee,
          And try my luck
At this new hand, the book upon my thighs,
        The word I should revise,

Tilted to me, by one of my two sons,
        The other, hooded, at
           My straining back:
          Laocoön's
Contrapposto is a bit like me
        Straining for my tea

Or hard notebook, wild-haired like him at dawn.
The corresponding heart
In this hard art
Is but a stone
Once stumbled on, as a few songs' strewn bits
Are these lines' caryatids.

My heavy hand is on the page, his cunning
Fingers, in behind
The inside spine,
Touch the running
Heads: this song's supporting song, its rock
In whom my form is locked.

The other child is breathing at my ear
Fresh sounds for our old words,
Often misheard
By me, quite clear
To him, and like an empty simile
Their shadow crosses me.

145 ❧ Hermes
Of David

As at the end of all creation,
Inside my living room's door-frame,
There must he stand,
At his old game:
A toddler in great elation,
Unmaking the stringed instrument in hand.

'As for me, I'll be talking of
Thy majesty', I say he sings,
'Of wondrous works',
Or words, or things:
The furtive brightening love
Our youngest son now has for our dark words.

I put these words together in
A mildly urgent state, before
        He stirs and calls
        For me. The more
I meditate on him,
His cries for food and smiles, his quick footfalls,

        The more a future act, or word,
        Impacts upon my words, and makes
            Me pause above
            The spring that breaks
        This page, as if I heard
A kingdom break upward outside in love.

        'I will extol . . . thy name' in this
        Departure from the final song
            Ascribed to a shepherd.
            Voiceless for long,
        I watch these things of his
Declare now themselves colourfully upward.

146 ❧ The Rainbow
Hallelujah

A turbulent unruly thing of being
Walks in the room and kicks an orange pot,
            Triumphantly peeing
            At last, and not
Upon his scattered toys, to my amaze,
But where he should, to loud acclaim and praise.

I am enchanted and on edge at once,
Aware, recalling this scene, that there must be
            A force that wants,
            Reluctantly,
To learn the rules of praise in these lines too,
Declaring to me my thoughts as if I were you.

Happy is he whose hope is in that breath
'*Which* made heaven and earth', whose praise is that
'*Which* executeth
Judgment' as at
The end of time: that artist who hasn't got
Even a proverbial, or rainbow's, pot.

147 ❧ Celestial Spheres of Mistletoe
Hallelujah

A word was dropped throughout my head
And took its chances.
Soon spheres of gold and green were spread
On leafless branches
Like great expanses
Of virgin plains rolled backward through
Eternity
Into the stars and sun of a new
Reality.

The praise I want is like snow: my fire
Will make hoarfrost.
Wrapped in cold I will stand before
The cold: I will feast
On morsels of ice.
They say that Plato's but a poet
Disentangled:
Behold how my old tangled coat
Has come unraveled.

A Photophobic Man

Hallelujah

All things in themselves are a wild old air,
                    So weird and fine:
A supernatural strain of praise to their
                    Old friend and creator.
They are the strangest theme you ever heard,
                    Once upon a time,
To which you're bound to put some words, his word,
                    Sooner or later,
If you recall your dream of the opening line.

The stone complete in itself was cut and priced,
                    After the Fall,
The earth deforested and privatized,
                    And cattle bred
To graze upon it for our greedy table.
                    The world was all
Contention, consciousness at last unable
                    To see what's said
Of hosts of angels lined against the wall.

But then a courteous photophobic man
                    Roused himself
To lend his voice to dragons of the main,
                    All deeps in his gaze,
And made a canticle that crowned creation.
                    He struck and delved
Fresh courtly songs to make a transplantation
                    Of a Psalm of praise,
A tree, which spread like books upon a shelf.

149 ❧ Stained Glass

Hallelujah

The masons' esoteric marks,
        Mostly effaced,
     Below a lovingly
        Carved monkey's face,
Make me wonder if an ogee arch
    And flowing tracery—
The glass it used to hold when it was painted—
        Was praise enough
   To bring the men who put it up
   A life closer to being sainted.

Their work of praise remains in place
        Ahead of time
    And draws me in to stare.
       I find that I'm
Bound with chains and fetters of iron, faced
    With judgment everywhere
I look, a two-edged sword above my poor
        Ekphrastic book,
   Cutting away the time it took
   To make it, showing me the door.

150 ❧ The Firmament

Hallelujah

Westwards down the nave,
The end of evensong,
A choir of girls in green
Sang, 'Let every thing
That hath breath, praise the Lord',
And I grew cold and colder.
The old choirmaster twitched
In time over his shoulder
The hand that they all followed.
They went away and sent
Their little voices high
Inside the firmament.

The weeks before last Christmas
You sang throughout our house,
In lines, half-lines, and odd words,
A song you must have rehearsed
Over and over again
With friends at nursery:
'The angels are singing good news'.
It was the first time that we
Had ever heard you sing,
And it took me several days
To sit up and listen at last
To your fine example of praise.

Acknowledgements

I am grateful to the editors of the following magazines and journals where some of these poems appeared: *Archipelago, Cassandra Voices, The Deronda Review, E-Verse Radio, Neke: The New Zealand Journal of Translation Studies,* and *Spiritus.* I am most grateful to Anthony Caleshu for publishing *Eighteen Psalms* (Periplum Poetry, 2018), which provides a selection of poems from this book.

A few of these poems were first published on air in September 2018 on BBC Radio 4 in *Clarke's Psalter:* I am very grateful to Anna Scott-Brown and Adam Fowler for making this programme and to Paul Daniel Curran for reciting the poems. Andy Bancroft Cooke is producing an album of a selection of these poems set to music by Corrado Fantoni.

Thanks are due especially to Mark S. Burrows for his early and continued support of this book and for the invitation to give a reading from it at the 2017 Power of the Word Conference in Oxford; to Helen Appleton, Susan Gillingham and Francis Leneghan of the Oxford Psalms Network for inviting me to give a reading of some of these poems in May 2018; and to the organizers of the 2018 Church Times Festival of Poetry for inviting me to give a reading in Salisbury.

I would also like to thank my family, in particular, Francesca, Ludovico and Iacopo, and those who read versions of these poems along the way, especially Ned Denny, Ernest Hilbert, Jamie McKendrick, Nathaniel Mellors, Barry Ryan, Frank Armstrong, Avshalom Guissin, Susan Sorek, Alexander Massey, Thea Gomelauri, Enrico Racca, Jonathan Walton, Paul Downes, and Philip Coleman.

About Paraclete Press

Who We Are

As the publishing arm of the Community of Jesus, Paraclete Press presents a full expression of Christian belief and practice—from Catholic to Evangelical, from Protestant to Orthodox, reflecting the ecumenical charism of the Community and its dedication to sacred music, the fine arts, and the written word. We publish books, recordings, sheet music, and video/DVDs that nourish the vibrant life of the church and its people.

What We Are Doing

BOOKS | PARACLETE PRESS BOOKS show the richness and depth of what it means to be Christian. While Benedictine spirituality is at the heart of who we are and all that we do, our books reflect the Christian experience across many cultures, time periods, and houses of worship.

We have many series, including *Paraclete Essentials*; *Paraclete Fiction*; *Paraclete Poetry*; *Paraclete Giants*; and for children and adults, *All God's Creatures*, books about animals and faith; and *San Damiano Books*, focusing on Franciscan spirituality. Others include *Voices from the Monastery* (men and women monastics writing about living a spiritual life today), *Active Prayer*, and new for young readers: *The Pope's Cat*. We also specialize in gift books for children on the occasions of Baptism and First Communion, as well as other important times in a child's life, and books that bring creativity and liveliness to any adult spiritual life.

The MOUNT TABOR BOOKS series focuses on the arts and literature as well as liturgical worship and spirituality; it was created in conjunction with the Mount Tabor Ecumenical Centre for Art and Spirituality in Barga, Italy.

MUSIC | The PARACLETE RECORDINGS label represents the internationally acclaimed choir *Gloriæ Dei Cantores*, the *Gloriæ Dei Cantores Schola*, and the other instrumental artists of the *Arts Empowering Life Foundation*.

Paraclete Press is the exclusive North American distributor for the Gregorian chant recordings from St. Peter's Abbey in Solesmes, France. Paraclete also carries all of the Solesmes chant publications for Mass and the Divine Office, as well as their academic research publications.

In addition, PARACLETE PRESS SHEET MUSIC publishes the work of today's finest composers of sacred choral music, annually reviewing over 1,000 works and releasing between 40 and 60 works for both choir and organ.

VIDEO | Our video/DVDs offer spiritual help, healing, and biblical guidance for a broad range of life issues including grief and loss, marriage, forgiveness, facing death, understanding suicide, bullying, addictions, Alzheimer's, and Christian formation.

Learn more about us at our website:
www.paracletepress.com
or phone us toll-free at 1.800.451.5006

SCAN
TO
READ
MORE

You may also be interested in . . .

99 *Psalms* by Said
Translated from German by Mark S. Burrows
ISBN 978-1-61261-294-2 | $17.99

The Paraclete Poetry Anthology
Selected and New Poems
Edited by Mark S. Burrows
ISBN 978-1-61261-906-4 | $20

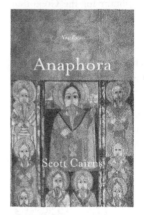

Anaphora
New Poems
Scott Cairns
ISBN 978-1-61261-838-8 | $18